TRAITOR

TRAITOR

A HISTORY OF AMERICAN BETRAYAL FROM
BENEDICT ARNOLD TO DONALD TRUMP

DAVID ROTHKOPF

THOMAS DUNNE
BOOKS
NEW YORK

First published in the United States by Thomas Dunne Books, an imprint of St. Martin's Publishing Group.

TRAITOR. Copyright © 2020 by David Rothkopf. All rights reserved. Printed in the United States of America. For information, address St. Martin's Publishing Group, 120 Broadway, New York, NY 10271.

www.thomasdunnebooks.com

Designed by Omar Chapa

Library of Congress Cataloging-in-Publication Data

Names: Rothkopf, David J. (David Jochanan), 1955- author.
Title: Traitor : a history of American betrayal from Benedict Arnold to
    Donald Trump / David Rothkopf.
Other titles: History of American betrayal from Benedict Arnold to
    Donald Trump
Description: First edition. | New York : Thomas Dunne Books, [2020] |
    Includes index.
Identifiers: LCCN 2020019386 | ISBN 9781250228833 (hardcover) |
    ISBN 9781250228840 (ebook)
Subjects: LCSH: Trump, Donald, 1946- | Treason—United States—
    History. | Traitors—United States—History. | Presidents—United
    States—History. | Presidents—Professional ethics—United States. |
    Presidents—United States—Conduct of life. | Character—Political
    aspects—United States. | United States—Politics and government—2017-
Classification: LCC E912 .R68 2020 | DDC 973.933092—dc23
LC record available at https://lccn.loc.gov/2020019386

Our books may be purchased in bulk for promotional, educational, or business use. Please contact your local bookseller or the Macmillan Corporate and Premium Sales Department at 1-800-221-7945, extension 5442, or by email at MacmillanSpecialMarkets@macmillan.com.

First Edition: 2020

10 9 8 7 6 5 4 3 2 1

For my mom,
whose last words, in response to a question
about how she felt about Donald Trump, were
"I hate him"

CONTENTS

TRAITOR

INTRODUCTION

THE GREATEST BETRAYAL IN AMERICAN HISTORY

Though those that are betray'd do feel the treason sharply, yet the traitor stands in worse case of woe.

—William Shakespeare, *Cymbeline*

The president of the United States is a traitor.

He is a liar. He is a fraud. He is a racist. He is a misogynist. He is incompetent. He is corrupt. He is unfit in almost every respect for the high office he holds.

But what distinguishes him from every other bad leader the United States has had and, indeed, from every other senior official of the U.S. government in over twenty-four decades of history, is that he has repeatedly, indisputably, and egregiously betrayed his country.

How that will be defined and litigated by prosecutors and by the Congress of the United States is a work in progress. Cases revealing the instances of his placing foreign interests before those of the United States, always ultimately to serve his own greed or personal ambition, will likely be surfacing for years to come. So may, too, the abuses of power or negligence that contributed to exacerbating the consequences of the worst public health crisis suffered by the U.S. in a century. But for historians and for students of facts that are already available to the public, there is no question Trump has met every necessary standard to define his behavior as traitorous. As his presidency has progressed, other scandals have manifested themselves, so many that they have blended together to sometimes obscure this core truth. But it has remained, and day to day his actions have manifested his willingness to serve any country that might help him personally whether that country was the one he was elected to lead or not.

At its core, that definition depends on breaking faith with the people of the country he was chosen to lead. But the story of his betrayals began long before he took office and then continued and was compounded by his actions as president. While we may not yet have uncovered many of his crimes, the story we know so far is so outrageous and disturbing that it raises, and I believe answers, a question that has never before been presented in American history: Has America's forty-fifth president been the greatest threat this country has faced during his tenure in office?

In 2016, during the presidential campaign ultimately won by Trump by the thinnest of margins and with the aid of Vladimir Putin and the intelligence services of the Russian Federation, I was serving as the editor of *Foreign Policy* magazine. At that time, knowing of the ties of Trump and the team around him to the Russians, his solicitation of Russian aid, his embrace of Russian positions, his propensity for corruption, his repeated lies and deceptions about his links to Russia, and his deeply flawed character, my colleagues and I made a decision unprecedented in the almost half-century-long history of the magazine.

We wrote an editorial urging against the election of Trump and asserting that the risk his elevation to the presidency would pose would be grave.

We were not alone. The warning signs were there. More than that, he had not only made public his embrace of Russian assistance with his objective of defeating Hillary Rodham Clinton, but we knew that the Russians were using active measures to attack the United States. (In fact, we at *Foreign Policy* had been among those attacked by "Fancy Bear," the Russian hackers later demonstrated by Robert Mueller's team to be part of a Russian military-intelligence-team effort to hack not only the Democratic National Committee—DNC—but a number of sites they felt might be influential in the United States, including, in addition to *Foreign Policy*, the Council on Foreign Relations and others.) It was known that Paul Manafort, Trump's campaign chairman, had shady ties to Russian oligarchs, including some very close to Vladimir Putin, and we had seen as Manafort and Trump's team had altered the GOP platform to take a more Russia-friendly stance on Ukraine despite Russia's serial violations of international laws and norms in its attacks on that country and its seizure of Crimea.

In other words, these were not just political dirty tricks that Trump was engaged in. This was collaboration with one of America's most determined adversaries, the one country in the world that had more nuclear weapons than the United States.

Of course, since Trump took office, the scope and scale of his cooperation with the Russians and their consequences came into clearer focus, and campaign crimes were compounded by crimes committed to obstruct justice to protect not just Trump and his team but the Russians, too. In fact, throughout Trump's first term of office, he has repeatedly undertaken actions that protect Russia and Russians, advanced their interests, and thwarted the efforts of the U.S. intelligence, law-enforcement, diplomatic, and military communities as they sought to stop or counteract Russian wrongdoing. He has also sought the involvement of other governments in helping to serve his personal objectives, from Ukraine to China, placing personal interests above national interests, another form of grave betrayal. And, as of this writing, despite the multiple investigations into the president's activities and the serial revelations of his misdeeds and a formal congressional impeachment investigation, Donald Trump shows no signs of reversing or even moderating these efforts. Indeed, as the Ukraine and China instances reveal, he entered into his campaign for reelection as he did his first campaign—soliciting aid from foreign powers to help him win power at home and offering to them the benefits of his holding that office. This approach echoes the "Trump first" ideology at the core of all he does. See, for example, how he denied or delayed federal assistance during the coronavirus outbreak to states whose governors he saw as being critical or even not fully appreciative of his efforts. That, too, was a betrayal of his duty to his country.)

Even after the Mueller investigation into his 2016 ties with the Russians and the Trump impeachment hearings which centered around his abuse of power in shaking down the Ukrainian government in order to advance his personal political interests, much remains to be revealed by the investigations into the president's involvement in and support of attacks against the United States, investigations that might not even be fully possible until he is out of office and those who are actively protecting him, from his attorney general to the Senate majority leader, are out of power or substantially weakened. But as of now, it is already clear that Russia's interference in our election and Russia's support of Trump has advanced major Russian objectives, including but not limited to unprecedented efforts by the U.S. president to weaken NATO and attack NATO allies; support for Russian positions in Syria; undercutting the standing of the United States in the world; fostering deep divisions within the United States; enabling further Russian cyber interventions in the United States; covering up past such interventions; embracing Russian leaders and representatives; supporting Russian efforts in Europe to promote right-wing nationalists who seek to undermine the European Union (EU); undoing sanctions against key Russian leaders, including those associated with the Russian invasion of Ukraine; and slow-walking other such sanctions or benefits to Russian rivals. Further, these goals have not just been achieved, they have been advanced by the president working in conjunction with a political party, the GOP, which has largely embraced Trump's pro-Russia stance as its own and which is complicit with the president and the Russians in advancing the goals mentioned.

It is hard to imagine that the Russians ever felt their efforts to support a fringe and unlikely candidate for the U.S. presidency would produce such immense successes for them. Even were Donald Trump removed from office tomorrow or should he be defeated in November 2020, the Russian achievements have been so great that their efforts to put him in office and use him to advance their goals has to be seen as perhaps the most successful international intelligence operation of modern times.

Much has been written about Trump and about this case. Important, compelling books have been published that detail why he should be impeached, that enumerate his crimes, that reveal his character flaws and his incompetence as well as those of the friends and political advisors around him. But there is a special need to understand Trump's betrayal from national-security and foreign policy perspectives. After all, Trump is the only president in American history to have been impeached on national security grounds.

Beyond that, the damage done has been so great and the threats remaining are so profound that it is our duty as citizens to understand how they came to be and what their potential long-term significance is. This means, above all, gaining historical context, understanding where Trump-Russia ranks among the acts of treachery committed by Americans against America since the country was born over 240 years ago. We also need to understand how the country has historically viewed such crimes and how it has treated them in the past to place what has happened in perspective.

Those are the reasons for this book. It is conceived to be a brief, fact-based review of past instances of betrayal and corruption that tries to rise above the political fray and the heated rhetoric and that considers the abuses of Donald Trump from the perspective of history and of our future security. In other words, it is not looking as much at the nature of Trump—rightfully the focus of much attention—as it is at the nature and the potential costs to the United States of the betrayal. It is not looking at the legalities of treason or conspiracy against the United States or espionage laws as much as it is what happens when the president of the United States places loyalty to another country or self-interest (that in turn benefits him by benefiting some foreign actor) before his duty to his own.

Trump is despicable, the least of us. But beyond his defective or perhaps even nonexistent character, there are the near-term and lasting consequences of his actions. We must understand these to reverse them, and we must understand how easily Russia achieved its objectives in order to prevent further such catastrophes in the future.

As we will see, while having a president who is a traitor is unprecedented, there have been many Americans in our history who have, for money or ambition, misjudgment or spite, turned their backs on our flag and people. These offenses started early in the history of our nation. In fact, the concept of loyalty to a cause or country meant more to the founders because the tumultuous formative years of American history were so riven by plots and intrigues. When young George Washington made his first military forays during the French and Indian War, it was often unclear whose side indigenous tribes were on, and one of Washington's initial defeats was marked by his signing an agreement with the French granting him and his troops free passage on terms so odious that its translator was for a period accused of treason, of betraying the British Crown, for whom Washington was fighting. Of course, the revolution itself also saw treachery and betrayal— and even some of those who appeared for a time to be fighting for American independence were themselves accused of being traitors to the king. The story of Benedict Arnold, once a trusted general and friend of Washington's, is now taught to every schoolchild in the country and, indeed, is likely the very first incident most Americans think of when they hear the word "traitor."

Arnold, of course, gave sensitive military information to the British and later fought alongside them, which is as clear a case of betraying the fledgling country as there could be. But when you ask how different it is from working with an adversary government when it is seeking to attack via a modern means— information warfare—the core institutions of American democracy, or later embracing policies on behalf of foreign sponsors that weaken and even seek the destruction of vital American alliances and to enhance the strategic position of enemies, even this first most egregious betrayal of Arnold's does not seem so distant or different from what we have witnessed in our own time. Similarly, betraying foreign allies from Ukraine to Kurdistan, putting our vital interests at grave risk or, alternatively, looking the other way when a foreign potentate might murder an American journalist, all to advance his personal political or financial needs, carry with them echoes of past abuses, including many which were not so egregious as Trump's.

As we shall see in the first chapter of this book, the early years of the United States were marked by constant accusations of disloyalty between Federalists, who were accused of being too close to Britain; Jeffersonians, who were viewed as being too close to France; and all manner of plots and scandals associated with these divisions. Aaron Burr, Thomas Jefferson's vice president, better known today as the man who killed Alexander Hamilton in a duel, was even part of a plot to form his own nation in among the territories of the Spanish in Louisiana and Mexico. He was arrested for treason in February of 1807 but was not convicted because of the constitutional requirement that treason require an "overt act," the kind of technicality often used in Trump's defense today. Burr, however, was viewed as a traitor the rest of his life, and he was forced to spend a number of years in Europe in exile before returning to New York to practice law, a profession apparently then as now open to people of dubious repute.

In the centuries since, the United States has witnessed outright sedition and the treason that brought about the Civil War, but even then, while a number of leaders of the Confederacy—from Jefferson Davis to Robert E. Lee—had held senior positions in the U.S. federal government, none, of course, operated at the level of Trump as president. In the past century, traitors have more often been prosecuted under espionage laws because the legal bar set to prove treason has been set so high, but there is no doubt that spies from the Rosenbergs to Aldrich Ames and Robert Hanssen were ultimately seen as traitors regardless of the terms of their convictions.

Understanding this history is key because it provides legal as well as historical context in which to view the Trump case. But in the course of the book, we will also seek to define and explore the other elements of the story vital to understanding its national-security implications. These include considering the moment in history in which the Trump betrayals have taken place, the key actors in undertaking those betrayals (because this is indeed a conspiracy that extends far beyond the president and his immediate family), the charges that have been made against Trump and those close to him, and the consequences of the betrayal. In addition, we need to further understand the nature of modern warfare and why old definitions—while operative in legal definitions of what makes an "enemy"—may be misleading and provide cover for our adversaries at home and abroad.

It is also vital to understand the politics of our time not just because they created the opening for Trump but because they created a wall of defense behind which he and his coconspirators could act, thanks to the active complicity of the GOP leadership, the Republican-led Senate (and, for the first two years of Trump's presidency, of the House of Representatives), and the penetration of Russian actors and money into the financing apparatus of the GOP and related organizations like the National Rifle Association (NRA). These things in turn created the sense of opportunity Trump saw in every foreign interaction, viewing them each in a personal, transactional light, as deals that he might strike for his benefit or to the detriment of his enemies.

That will be the path this short volume will take. But it is my conviction that, upon reviewing the facts, the only objective conclusion that can be drawn is that wittingly or otherwise, Donald Trump; those closest to him in his White House, his campaign, and his family; and the leaders of the Republican Party in the United States have committed the highest-level, greatest, most damaging betrayal in the history of the country. They are traitors. And as of this writing they continue to damage the United States as no other actors in the world can.

Indeed, even a passing review of the facts can only lead to the conclusion that the greatest threat the United States has faced since the end of the Cold War is Donald Trump and his allies in the government, most notably Senator Mitch McConnell and the Republican leadership, working in support of and defense of the anti-U.S. objectives and initiatives of Russian president Vladimir Putin.

Some have called it the greatest scandal in American history. But that hardly does it justice. Unaddressed and unacknowledged, it could be the plot that brought down the greatest force for freedom and justice the world has ever known, the post–World War II Western alliance led by the United States of America. It could also, through the abuses of the presidents and his supporters and the techniques by which they both grabbed for power and sought to defend themselves, lead to the undoing of American democracy. Two and a half centuries after Benedict Arnold sought to ensure that America remained in a tyrant's grasp, Donald Trump and his foreign sponsors may well have advanced that objective as Arnold could not.

I

BETRAYAL

The first duty of society is justice.

—Alexander Hamilton

History is the highest court. Its jurisdiction knows no boundaries. Its final verdict cannot be appealed.

When we leave justice to the courts or to legislatures or even to the prevailing public opinion of a moment, we are only taking the first steps in preparing the case for posterity to weigh. History's judgment cannot be rushed. Its deliberations are often torturously slow, and their ebb and flow can shift with generations. But ultimately a decision is handed down. Ultimately each era and each actor within it is assessed.

It is hard in a time such as ours, tumultuous and fraught, to have the perspective to see what time may weigh as important or frivolous. This is especially so in an era in which entire industries exist to spin the latest headlines into opinions or, better yet, controversies. The goal of most of our debates is not light but heat, not understanding but ratings, or to score political points.

Emotion is the outcome demagogues and many television executives prefer to insight or perspective.

This has never been clearer than in the coverage and assessments generated by the campaign and presidency of Donald Trump. To some of us, from the outset Trump represented a danger to the United States, our values, our institutions, our standing in the world, and to many of the most vulnerable among our people. To others this perceived threat was a fabrication that triggered a "witch hunt" and "fake news."

With each new development—from Trumpian statements or tweets intended to shock, distract, or entertain, to exposés of alleged crimes, to announcements of investigations into the president, his family, or his allies and even then, to his impeachment and trial—America grew more divided about what was happening. Trump and his defenders asserted his innocence and hailed his achievements. His critics warned of the damage he was doing or the deficits in his character.

Subsequently, as preliminary judgments were rendered or sidestepped by courts or by the investigation of Special Counsel Robert Mueller, by the Department of Justice, or by the United States Congress, each side sought to claim victory and to interpret the conclusions as material, dispositive, or even final.

At the time of this book's writing, of course, investigations are ongoing, some still not well known to us, and still others seem possible. Some may have to wait until Trump leaves office.

Many years will pass before we can know for sure how the many accusations against the president and those close to him will play out in legal forums. But the facts of the cases we are familiar with are now much clearer—thanks to the work of Robert Mueller and his team, of journalists, and of congressional investigators like Representative Adam Schiff and the House Permanent Select Committee on Intelligence and Representative Jerry Nadler and the House Judiciary Committee. Surely more will come out. But we do finally have enough at hand to begin to assess how Trump and his administration may be seen by history.

That may seem to be a paradox. It may seem odd that even as matters are just beginning to be digested by the courts, legislators, and the American public, we might actually be able to draw some conclusions into how history might assess this period. But that is because the matters on the docket of history are not legal or technical. They turn on bigger, broader concepts. While history can be arbitrary, and while it is often, as the saying goes, "written by the victors," there are also patterns in history, especially around some of the core questions at issue in the case of President Trump, the Trump campaign, the Trump administration, and the other organizations run by Trump in his lifetime.

History is a helpful guide because we can take some of the central accusations made against Trump and we can see how the facts underlying the Trump case as we know them today weigh compared to the facts of past cases in American history. We can look for analogies and patterns that can give us the perspective that is sadly lacking from so many of our fevered debates or the scorched-earth exchanges of social media. We can look for those moments that, to paraphrase a quote often but wrongly attributed to Mark Twain, "rhyme" with past roughly similar events.

It's not an exact science. But it can be revealing, and at the very least it can put today's news cycles into some kind of useful context.

It is especially worthwhile given that so many of the assertions made about the Trump presidency are often accompanied by pronouncements that invoke history for comparative purposes. I will leave it for others to consider some of those—such as Trump's repeated assertions that he is the best president of all time or that his administration is the most productive in history or that we are enjoying the greatest economy in the history of the world. If you detect from my tone that I consider such things ridiculous and not worthy of your time or mine, you would be right. Besides, there are enough Trump hagiographers hard at work feeding the printing presses and websites and airwaves of America's right wing, that I'm sure that you will soon have access to titles comparing him to Pericles or perhaps promising to expound upon "what George Washington could learn from Donald Trump." (After all, there is an entire subgenre of art shared on the internet that depicts Trump with Jesus at his side or even as Jesus. So looney blasphemies already abound.)

Instead, what seems more important to the decisions the people of the United States have yet to make about Trump and his allies in and outside the U.S. government is determining how future generations might judge the weightiest accusations about him based on what we already know to be true.

Central to those accusations is one in particular: that during his presidential campaign and throughout his term of office, Donald Trump betrayed his country. This is different from whether or not he and those around him were corrupt, although some of that corruption—placing his interests or those of his family ahead of the country—certainly also does amount to a form of betrayal about which our founders were deeply and rightfully concerned. It is also different from whether Trump "colluded" with Russians or whether there was a "quid pro quo" in his 2019 dealings with the Ukrainian government of Volodymyr Zelensky, to use the terms promoted by Trump and his team, preferred precisely because they were vague or hard to prove or largely legally meaningless. It is also different from whether he or those close to him "conspired" with a foreign government, something Mueller felt he could not prove, whether due to obstruction of his investigation by Trump and those close to him or because it was difficult to prove that most or many of the more than one hundred meetings Trump's team had with Russians were actually with representatives of the Russian government. Finally, it is apart from an evaluation of his other failings and betrayals of his oath—from putting children in cages to denying aid to Puerto Rico, from undermining the rule of law to denying science and letting his personal politics set the stage for the pain and loss of the Covid-19 epidemic.

It is possible to betray your country without technically violating campaign finance laws or statutes against conspiring against the U.S. government or espionage laws. (It is also possible that Trump and his associates did all those things.). In fact, it has happened before in American history. What is involved is placing personal self-interest ahead of duty or a sworn oath or the expectation of loyalty that we have of every citizen, especially of those in high office. That can take the form of accepting campaign assistance from a foreign government that publicly espouses that one of its top priorities is to weaken the United States, or it can mean placing a vital ally in jeopardy to achieve a personal political benefit, as in Ukraine. (Without knowing more about Trump's finances and those of his family, of course, we can only speculate how many times this has happened. Did it happen when he sided with Turkey and Russia against the Kurds? With the Saudis when they murdered Jamal Khashoggi? With the Chinese? Time will surely tell as facts are made public.)

TREASON?

Words matter. Terms like "treason" have been tossed carelessly about in the conversation concerning Trump. For some, the confusion regarding the use of the word is quite natural. They are not familiar with the carefully worded provisions placed in the Constitution by its framers on the subject. To them, "Treason against the United States," as defined in Article III, Section 3, "shall consist only in levying War against them, or in adhering to their Enemies, giving them Aid and Comfort. No Person shall be convicted of Treason unless on the Testimony of two Witnesses to the same overt Act, or on Confession in open Court."

Reasonable and patriotic Americans could see a president who openly sought the help of a foreign enemy to win an election, embraced the aid of that enemy in the form of a direct attack on our democratic institutions, defended that enemy, and then rewarded that enemy with not only policies but with efforts to actually draw back defenses to make future attacks possible, and say, that's "adhering" to an enemy, that's "giving them Aid and Comfort." But others who have done the same have not been convicted of treason because the law has determined that in order to be an enemy, that country must be in a state of war declared against them by the United States. And still others who have provided aid and comfort to enemies have been acquitted or avoided charges because there were not two witnesses to a specific "overt act."

Treason carries with it a sentence of death. As a consequence, such technicalities surely matter. That is even the case in a country in which the president himself has used the term recklessly and without regard for the facts or established law—as Trump did when accusing the FBI investigators and members of the special counsel's team, who examined ties between Trump and his campaign and the Russians, of the crime.

But the absence of a case for treason, just like the absence of one for conspiracy against the United States, does not mean that something deeply disturbing and threatening to the well-being of the country did not happen. It does not mean that the president could not legitimately be described as traitorous. The dictionary definition of a traitor is "a person who betrays a friend, country or principle."

If, as was asserted by Robert Mueller, a foreign adversary— the Russians—undertook "multiple, systematic efforts to interfere in our election" and if that attack on our democracy was, as Mueller and other investigators have found, explicitly to harm one candidate, Hillary Clinton, and to benefit another, Donald Trump, and if Trump embraced the action of this adversary, celebrated it publicly, encouraged it in private, and then later both defended the attackers and rewarded them for their efforts through an unprecedented shift in U.S. policy toward them, it is hard not to see that as a serious, damaging betrayal. While his actions as a candidate were disloyal to his country, his actions as president to deny that the betrayal took place, to defend the attackers, and to obstruct the investigation into the Russian attack (thus making future attacks more likely) were even more serious kinds of wrong.

Each president takes an oath, saying "I do solemnly swear (or affirm) that I will faithfully execute the Office of President of the United States, and will to the best of my Ability, preserve, protect and defend the Constitution of the United States." That oath of course, binds the president to protecting the nation and the democratic institutions created by the Constitution and the laws of the country. It may be an impeachable offense to violate that oath. But that requires action by the Congress that is influenced by political realities that may or may not produce just outcomes. That said, the oath is the oath, and the actions of the president are the actions of the president, and so history will, congressional action or none, certainly judge the man's actions by the promises he made.

To understand how history will judge Trump, though, we must consider the past cases that are most like his—cases of betrayal, of men and women accused of being traitors, of the verdicts in the court of public opinion and how they may differ from those taken in courts of law or by the Congress. And there are many such cases.

WHAT DONALD TRUMP COULD LEARN FROM GEORGE WASHINGTON

It was a time of scandal, bitter political infighting, partisanship, personal attacks, betrayals, foreign intrigues, spies, plots, and calls to impeach the president. I'm not speaking of the past two years, but rather of a moment that has for many of us faded into the monochrome of woodcuts or pictures of larger-than-life heroes carved in relief onto white marble. I'm speaking of the first years of the United States and of our founders, who, after all, were only men—and men much more like those of today than we might like to admit.

In fact, as we shall see in the course of this book, every single issue that dominates today's headlines, every single debate, was presaged by the people and events that midwifed the United States into existence. In addition to those just cited, there were accusations of the existence of a kind of "deep state" cabal, there were partisan intrigues that trafficked in "fake news," there were truly bad men in it exclusively for themselves, and there was a sense that, unchecked, the scandals and divisions of the era could leave the country permanently broken.

That is not to say that the men of that era were the same as those of today. (Though, then as now, it was mostly men, and back then almost exclusively white men and men of means.) First, unlike today, there was greatness afoot; true giants, not just of U.S. history but world history, were making contributions that would change the nature of global society. Next, there were certainly different ethical and social expectations afoot—for better or for worse. And our first leaders were also unburdened by precedent or established U.S. law, so it must be acknowledged that they were feeling their way through this business of establishing a new nation, the first true large-scale democracy in the history of the world, entirely shed of any vestige of feudalism or aristocracy.

Indeed, the situation we are in today is arguably different from that faced by the founders in several important ways. First and foremost perhaps is that at the center of the government today we find a man who is unlike any other U.S. leader in our history. He is the only president never to have devoted one minute of his life to public service prior to taking office.

Flip through the pages of history. It doesn't take long to establish this fact. Washington served as the commanding officer of the Continental Army during the Revolutionary War. Adams chaired the committee charged with writing the Declaration of Independence and as vice president before he became president. Jefferson was the principal author of that declaration and served as secretary of state before becoming president. Madison was principal author of the Constitution and also served as secretary of state. Monroe, too, was the country's senior cabinet officer and chief diplomat, among his many accomplishments in public life prior to becoming the country's chief executive (as is true of all of this cohort of leaders except one). John Quincy Adams was another former secretary of state. Andrew Jackson—the only president to be censured by the Congress—had been a senator and a general. Martin Van Buren had been vice president. William Henry Harrison was a former general and diplomat. John Tyler was another who had served as vice president. James K. Polk was a former governor of Tennessee. Zachary Taylor had been a general. Millard Fillmore was a vice president and member of Congress. Franklin Pierce was a general, senator, and congressman. James Buchanan, a rival of Trump for worst-president honors, had been minister to the Court of St. James's in the United Kingdom, a senator, and a congressman. Abraham Lincoln had been a congressman. His successor, Andrew Johnson, the first president to be impeached by the House of Representatives, had been vice president and a senator, a governor, and a member of the House of Representatives. Ulysses S. Grant led U.S. forces in the Civil War. Rutherford B. Hayes was also a general and a congressman and a governor. James A. Garfield had also commanded forces in battle as a general and served as a member of Congress. Chester A. Arthur, whose experience prior to coming to Washington was pretty meager—he had a patronage job as collector of customs for the Port of New York—nonetheless did later serve as vice president before becoming president.

Grover Cleveland had been a governor of New York (and of course, had served as president prior to being the only man to reenter the White House for a second, nonconsecutive term). Benjamin Harrison had been a senator, and William McKinley a governor. Theodore Roosevelt had been a governor and then vice president. William H. Taft was secretary of war before becoming president (and later served as chief justice, the only man to head two different branches of the U.S. government). Woodrow Wilson was governor of New Jersey, Warren G. Harding a senator, Calvin Coolidge a governor and then vice president. Herbert Hoover, often cited as a business leader who became president, served as secretary of commerce prior to ascending to the White House. Franklin D. Roosevelt was assistant secretary of the navy and governor of New York. Harry S. Truman was a senator and FDR's last vice president. Dwight D. Eisenhower had been supreme Allied commander, John F. Kennedy a member of Congress and a senator. Lyndon B. Johnson had been a congressman, a senator, and vice president, as was Richard M. Nixon. Gerald R. Ford was a congressman and vice president, James Earl Carter governor of Georgia, and Ronald Reagan was governor of California. George H. W. Bush had been a congressman, an ambassador, Central Intelligence Agency (CIA) director, and vice president. William J. Clinton had been attorney general and governor of Arkansas. George W. Bush had been governor of Texas. Barack H. Obama had been an Illinois legislator and a senator.

It is, in my view, worth slogging through that list to see just what an aberration Donald Trump is from all his predecessors. But the lack of experience does not fully illustrate the difference in character between him and the men who came before him. That is illustrated, as we will see in the pages to come, by profound flaws in his character and judgment. As a consequence, even as we look, as we should, to history to provide us perspective, we should be careful from the outset to avoid false equivalencies. Indeed, our mission over the course of the remainder of this book should be to identify them, to distinguish not just what might be similar between now and the past, but also what is very different.

Let's look at four areas (all of which we will explore in greater depth as the book unfolds.) They are (1) the role of the "deep state" and intrigues, (2) controversies over dual loyalties, (3) America's first encounters with the idea of impeachment, and (4) real-life traitors and betrayal.

EVERYTHING STARTED WITH THE "DEEP STATE"

To the Europeans who were settling the British colonies in America, the country was a frontier. While indigenous people had been present for tens of thousands of years, the American Revolution broke out only about a century and a half after the first English settlers arrived, just a generation or two after most of the would-be leaders of the young country had ventured across the ocean at great risk to make their fortunes there. It was George Washington's great-grandfather who had been the first in his family to come to the United States. The Adamses arrived in Massachusetts Bay Colony a few years earlier, in 1636. Benjamin Franklin's father was born in England and emigrated in 1683. Thomas Paine was born in England, Alexander Hamilton in Nevis in the British Caribbean.

The country was sparsely populated. At the time Washington's family arrived on the continent, there were just over fifty thousand colonists. One hundred years later or so, the colonies passed the 1-million-person mark. Even at the time of the first U.S. census in 1790, that population was under 4 million people, roughly the size of present-day Oklahoma. The cities in which American history was made were not much more than small towns. The biggest of them, New York, home to Hamilton and Burr, had about 33,000 people during America's first years, about the size of the undergraduate enrollment at the University of Alabama today. Franklin's Philadelphia had 28,500. The Boston of the Adamses had just 18,000. To put that in perspective, Boston then was less than the population of two high-rise blocks in Manhattan today.

Virtually every fortune these individuals had was hard won, wrested from the land at great costs with few comforts, by modern standards. Combine this challenging environment and the kind of spirit that it took to be among those who were willing to embrace it—whether motivated by necessity or aspiration— and you have a would-be nation of tough characters.

That was, of course, manifest in the fact that as the British government sought to exploit those colonists through increasingly burdensome taxes while giving them virtually no say in the management of the new society they were carving at high cost from the challenging territory they sought to settle (or win from the Native Americans, whose homeland they sought to steal), and they chose to fight back. They chose to pit their tiny cluster of colonies on the edge of a wild continent against the most powerful nation on earth. Their leaders chose revolution despite the fact that failure would mean hanging for many and misfortune for their families.

These factors—being families of pioneers, living in harsh conditions, being used to taking great risks, and having a hard-won sense of a right to independence—were vital in contributing to the victory the colonists ultimately won over the British. But they also helped forge a generation of leaders who were tough, calculating, masters of fomenting political support for their positions, and unafraid of confrontation or worse.

That is very different from the conditions that have produced the leaders of today. The founders were used to fighting for survival, and each had many moments in their lives when all they had was at risk of being lost. While most of today's

political elites were not raised used to the luxuries and excesses
that marked the development of young Donald Trump, they all
grew up in the richest and most powerful country in the world,
and almost all ultimately found themselves competing not for
survival but for ever-increasing abundance.

So when we ask whether the early days of our Republic saw
the same kind of infighting, betrayals, and political maneuver-
ing that we see today, we have to remember that appearances
can be deceiving. The leaders of each period were shaped by
their times; their characters and their views of their allies and
rivals were formed under very different circumstances. And yet
the echoes between these times are chilling in what they illustrate about power—and vital to understand if we are to know
how we arrived at the system we have today, what our founders
feared for their countries future, why they feared, and how our
present situation is a manifestation of their worst nightmares of
a U.S. government run amok.

For example, just as Donald Trump and his supporters spin
stories of a "deep state" that is out to persecute Trump, we find
that they are tapping into the kind of conspiracy theories that
have always been with the United States (and most other societies). In fact, some argued back at the Republic's dawning that our
venerated Constitution itself and the new government it served
to shape and guide were the products of the secret machinations
of a would-be governing class, one that was founded to wield
power over common citizens on behalf of a power-hungry elite.

The birth of this conspiracy theory took place in the humble surroundings of Newburgh, New York, during the spring
of 1783. There, at Verplanck House, at the headquarters of General Friedrich Wilhelm von Steuben—a Prussian professional
soldier who had come to America to help school and lead the

Continental Army struggling to rise above its humble roots in colonial militias that were often not well organized, equipped, or trained—a meeting of a handful of senior officers took place.

The British surrender at Yorktown had taken place two years earlier. Now the army's leaders were considering their future. First and foremost, they were angry that the Continental Congress had not been keeping up its financial obligations to the army. Many of those even in the top ranks of the army were in dire financial straits. Washington's greatest task in the immediate aftermath of the war was quelling the growing unrest in the army related to these issues. Mutiny was in the air. Washington was forced into pleading with the Congress to do what was right.

Further, the army was about to be largely disbanded, and the futures of its leaders were not only under a financial cloud but many were worried they would fall out of touch, lose the connections and the spirit that had helped them win one of the most improbable victories the world had ever seen until that point. One of the organizers of this meeting in the Hudson River Valley was Major General Henry Knox. He had an idea: the creation of an organization consisting of the officers of the Continental Army who had served in the revolution.

His idea was heavily influenced by European orders of knights and nobility. It would be hereditary, the right to membership passed on to the firstborn sons of the former officers. Members would receive ribbons and medallions symbolizing their role, which they could wear with their dress uniforms. They would meet in independent chapters, organized state by state, with one for the foreign officers, mostly from France, who fought at their side. They would call themselves the Society of the Cincinnati, drawing their name from that of Cincinnatus, a

Roman leader who left his farm to lead Rome at a time of crisis, and who then, when he completed his task, turned down offers to become a ruler in order to return to his life as a farmer.

Naturally, the group picked George Washington as its leader, and Washington accepted the role. He would come to regret the decision. But before that happened, twenty-four hundred former officers had joined the group, including many names who would later further distinguish themselves in positions of leadership.

Within months, in the fall of 1783, discomfort with the idea began to manifest itself. A lawyer from South Carolina who had fought in the revolution, named Aedanus Burke, born in Ireland and deeply distrustful of the ways of societies he had seen in Britain, wrote a pamphlet under the pseudonym "Cassius," in which he suggested that the real purpose of the society was to create a new American nobility. "The Order is planted in a fiery, hot ambition, and thirst for power;" he wrote, "and its branches will end in tyranny."

The pamphlet stirred a controversy across the new country, a country also struggling with getting on its feet and doing so with the weak government established by the Articles of Confederation. Other pamphlets and debates followed. Some suggested the group could shape and influence outcomes in the fledgling Republic in dangerous ways. Indeed, many were concerned that was the primary purpose for its existence.

Washington was made very uncomfortable by the controversy. Jefferson sought to persuade him to give up his ties to the organization and that the society should be broken up. Others sent similar messages to Washington, including the Marquis de Lafayette, who was not comfortable with the hereditary nature of the honor that membership in the society bestowed. As a result, Washington sought major revisions in the group's charter, to do away with anything that appeared to be creating a kind of quasi nobility.

He won agreement at a general meeting of the society in 1784 to have the changes made (although ultimately they were not implemented due to a resistance by membership chapters in some states to ratify them). And he felt the controversy had been managed. But the country continued to stumble along under the Articles of Confederation, and some of the articles' most acute critics, such as Alexander Hamilton, were members of the society. As it happened, the next major meeting of the society was scheduled to take place in Philadelphia in 1787, at precisely the same time a Constitutional Convention was convening to reconsider the United States' fledgling system of government. Washington was invited to preside over both meetings. Although he, ever Cincinnati-like, sought to avoid either role, he was ultimately persuaded to do both. The meeting of the society was reported to be uneventful. The new Constitution was drafted and, as it turned out, the first president was Washington, and of his new cabinet members, Knox became his secretary of war, Hamilton his secretary of the treasury, and another member, Timothy Pickering, served as postmaster general, then secretary of war and secretary of state.

Needless to say, these coincidences were too much for many critics, who felt that despite Washington's efforts and protestations, the members of the society had effectively engineered the remaking of the government and their takeover of it. These assertions did not abate when Hamilton, later the head of the society, was suspected of using his connections within it to advance his views and ambitions. They did not even end when another member of the society, who also used its networks to his advantage, including founding a New York bank that rivaled one owned by Hamilton, shot and killed Hamilton on a bluff overlooking the Hudson in July of 1804.

In short, the birth of the country was accompanied by rumors of conspiracy and secret government and intrigue, which would seem perfectly in keeping with stories of the "deep state" spread today on Fox News or by Breitbart.

But the similarities with today go further. Because behind the stories of conspiracies lay the individual aspirations of men who sought power and of groups divided by ideology. The Constitution that was born in Philadelphia in 1787, did not anticipate the creation or evolution in the United States of political parties. But the battles that began to manifest themselves around debates like those associated with both the Constitution and the society were manifestations of tensions that would also create factions in the United States that in turn became parties, parties that behaved very similarly to those we have today—which is to say, badly, playing rough and dirty, blending and thus distorting heartfelt ideology with the ambitions and faults of their members.

FOUNDING RIVALS

Many of the men most closely associated with the Society of the Cincinnati, such as Washington and Hamilton, believed in a strong central government in the United States, in part because they saw the dangers of the weak government created by the Articles of Confederation. Some of them, like Hamilton, saw other benefits—from a better ability to create and manage the economy, to a fear of the potential for chaos and division in a government too much in the thrall of the masses. Others, many of them opponents of the Cincinnati (and some who were its members), feared that a strong central government would begin to concentrate power in the hands of the few and invite tyranny, such as that from which they had just wrestled themselves free. These men, led most notably by Jefferson, were proponents of the rights of states to have more autonomy in governing themselves. They also tended to represent the views of the agricultural South more, while the Federalists were more associated with the industrializing North.

Other divisions, in some cases more reflective of divisions of personal beliefs or ties, also played a big role in the divisions that pushed the parties apart. Jefferson had close ties to France. Hamilton, despite playing a leading role in the war with the English, still had strong affinities to the English. (Others, as we will see in the next chapter, sought to foster ties with Spain.) This was not only reflective of the newness of America but also of the shifting nature and constant competition for power in the world. France and England (and Spain and others) were seeking ties to the new nation, and some among them were facing, as in the case of France, massive internal upheaval, with which some Americans, such as Jefferson, were very sympathetic.

Meanwhile, the politics of the day was every bit as brutal and personal as today's. While our first leaders were spared the lunacies and excesses of social media or cable news, all the emotions of what has been called in our time the "blood sport" of politics were on display between the men and the incipient parties of this new nation. Media outlets became partisan tools, managed even more directly by the partisans than they are today.

During Washington's first term, the Federalists enjoyed the support in Philadelphia of a paper called the *Gazette of the United States*. Jefferson with his ally Madison sought an alternative and brought to Philadelphia a journalist named Philip Freneau. Freneau created and edited a Jeffersonian Republican (also known as Democratic-Republican) paper called the *National Gazette*, which existed for the purpose of attacking Hamilton and his allies, including Washington. This arrangement later created a scandal when it was revealed that Jefferson, in order to help support Freneau, had given him a job in the translation office at the State Department even though he spoke just one foreign language. And the government provided much of the income that in turn helped support Freneau's publication.

Similarly, toward the end of the first term of the Washington administration, another journalist and radical Republican attracted Jefferson's favor. His name was James T. Callender. He was a Scotsman who had come to Philadelphia and sought to make his name laying out a kind of political philosophy for the era that was more socially just and free from the pitfalls of European traditions. In so doing, he also began to attack the Federalists, whom he saw being drawn toward some of those traditions, among them Washington, his vice president, John Adams, and Alexander Hamilton.

While much of what Callender wrote was reasoned, frequently what he wrote took a lower route of attack. In 1797, for example, he exposed an affair Hamilton had with a woman named Maria Reynolds—America's first major sex scandal. Jefferson liked what he saw and later would support Callender to get him to attack John Adams, the man who succeeded Washington. At that time Jefferson was encouraging these attacks, it should be noted; he was a close colleague of the subjects of the attacks. He was secretary of state when Hamilton was secretary of the treasury, and when he promoted the attacks on President Adams, he was, in fact, Adams's vice president.

Adams would have none of this, and under the provisions of an attack on press freedom that would make Donald Trump's mouth water should he ever hear of it (or read a page of history), called the Sedition Act of 1798, he had Callender arrested for some of his antigovernment writings, notably a pamphlet of government corruption called *The Prospect Before Us*. Callender was convicted by a court overseen by Supreme Court Justice Samuel Chase, who, in another echo of today's times, was later impeached, in part for his involvement in the Callender trial. And in yet another bit of history that rhymes, Jefferson, when he became president in 1800, pardoned Callender.

What Jefferson did not do was accede to Callender's request that he then be made postmaster general of Richmond, Virginia. This may have been a matter of principle for Jefferson, though given the behavior we have noted earlier and that we shall soon see, such matters were not a hallmark of Jefferson's public service. Callender's response was to publish letters revealing that he, like Freneau, had been on Jefferson's payroll. Jefferson's supporters responded in the spirit of the high political discourse of the era by saying Callender's wife had died of a venereal disease he gave her.

Callender's response was then to publish, beginning in September 1802, a series of articles describing Jefferson's relations with one of his slaves, Sally Hemings. It was racist and despicable, and when it did not sufficiently turn public opinion against the then president, Callender went on to allege other infidelities by Jefferson.

It all seems eerily familiar and repugnant, doesn't it? It suggests that these were men who pulled no punches (and of course we have yet to get to the dispute between Jefferson's vice president and the leader of Democratic-Republicans in New York

State—Aaron Burr and Hamilton—or the one between Burr and the entirety of the United States that followed that.) It is a far cry from the exalted image we have of these men as demigods or titans who strode the earth in some ancient, alternative reality.

It is because these men were acutely aware of the flaws of men, their susceptibility to corruption, and their general propensity toward frailty, that back in that summer of 1787, Madison and those with whom he crafted the Constitution made sure to include a provision that Congress could impeach high officials, including the president, and remove them from office. In a time of shifting loyalties, it also included provisions against treason. Indeed, everyone who crafted the Constitution saw the prospect of such betrayals from the unique perspective of having committed such treason against their sovereign just years before in the form of the American Revolution.

IMPEACH GEORGE WASHINGTON

In the very first article of the Constitution, the issue was therefore directly addressed. In Article I, Section 2, it specifies that "the House of Representatives . . . shall have the sole Power of Impeachment." Later in Article I, Section 3, it grants to the Senate:

> . . . the sole Power to try all Impeachments. When sitting for that Purpose, they shall be on Oath or Affirmation. When the President of the United States is tried, the Chief Justice shall preside: And no Person shall be convicted without the Concurrence of two thirds of the Members present.
>
> Judgment in Cases of Impeachment shall not extend further than to removal from Office, and disqualification to hold and enjoy any Office of honor, Trust or Profit under the United States: but the Party convicted shall nevertheless be

> *liable and subject to Indictment, Trial, Judgment and Punish-*
> *ment, according to Law.*

Later, in Article II, Section 4, it further elaborates:

> *The President, Vice President and all civil Officers of the*
> *United States, shall be removed from Office on Impeach-*
> *ment for, and Conviction of, Treason, Bribery, or other high*
> *Crimes and Misdemeanors.*

The Constitution is a relatively short document, very efficient in its use of language. That it devotes such prominence to
this issue is a sign that its writers felt it would arise.

It did not take long for this theory to be tested. William
Blount, a U.S. senator representing Tennessee, was the first person to be subject to the Constitution's provisions in this regard.
On July 8, 1797, the House of Representatives impeached him for
his secret efforts to help Great Britain seize Spanish-controlled
territories in areas that today would be part of Florida and Louisiana. He was not convicted by the Senate because that body
had already expelled him before his trial, and therefore it was
concluded the Senate no longer had jurisdiction. Later courts
would rule that members of the Congress could not be impeached at all.

But Blount was not the first person whose impeachment
was called for. That distinction fell to the nation's first president,
George Washington, and among those calling for his ouster to
be considered was his first secretary of state, Thomas Jefferson.
At this point, such behavior might not seem surprising for Jefferson (who was soon no longer on speaking terms with his
fellow Virginian.) And again we find that the core divisions of

partisanship and international loyalties of the country's leaders played a central role in this controversy.

The issue at stake was how to deal with renewed hostilities between the United States and Britain. The British were no longer honoring provisions of the peace treaty and were arming Native Americans to attack U.S. settlements on the frontier and attacking and encouraging attacks on U.S. vessels at sea. Pro-French Americans, like Jefferson, wanted to see the United States stand up again to the British. Others, like Hamilton, sought a negotiated solution.

Hamilton was among those who encouraged Washington to appoint emissaries to Britain to seek a treaty. The leader of the delegation was the first chief justice of the United States, John Jay (who, like Hamilton, was a New Yorker and, like Hamilton, had attended Kings College, later known as Columbia University). Jay came back with an agreement, and it was then that the political controversy started.

It was 1795. Washington was sixty-three. He had been buffeted by the trials faced by the new country, including, for the three preceding years, unrest in the form of the Whiskey Rebellion. He knew America was fragile. He was outraged at the British attacks but also understood the divisions within the country. He had seen them manifest up close in the constant battles between Hamilton and Jefferson. He had been a witness as they bickered. He had heard of Hamilton's attacks on Jefferson's "womanish attachment to France." He had watched as Jefferson orchestrated attacks on Hamilton, including, in the Republican-controlled House, seeking to impeach Hamilton for mismanagement of government funds—accusations Hamilton deftly defended himself against in the best possible way, by providing detailed, meticulous records of the accounts in his charge.

Jefferson went further, once suggesting that any Virginian who did business with Hamilton's Bank of the United States, the central bank on which many of his ambitious plans as secretary of the treasury turned, would be guilty of "treason."

Now, Washington had to manage all this and the British threat. He concluded that the best path would be to embrace the treaty negotiated by Jay, even though it contained some odious provisions. The worst of those could be excised. But he also knew the treaty would have to be kept under wraps or it would trigger a nationwide controversy.

The American government has always been leaky. It was leaky then as it is now. Word of the treaty got out, and within days they were burning Jay in effigy in cities across the country for capitulating to the British. Jay joked that he could walk from one end of the country to the other at night with his path lit by the effigies of himself in flames.

As allies of Jefferson and the Republicans got hold of a copy of the full text of the treaty and published it, the attacks grew and turned against even the venerated Washington. Virginians were drinking toasts to the "speedy death of General Washington." Washington managed to get the treaty passed by the Senate, thanks to the thin majority the Federalists maintained in that chamber, on strictly a party-line vote that would have made the likes of Mitch McConnell proud. But then a Republican senator gave the full text of the treaty to Benjamin Franklin's grandson, Benjamin Franklin Bache, who published it and a screed attacking it as "illegitimately begotten" and approved by "a secret lodge of Senators." (There's always a conspiracy theory.)

Jefferson, no longer secretary of state, attacked the treaty as "execrable" and as an "infamous act." He portrayed its acceptance as an act of cowardice, capitulation under threat of war.

Hamilton was stoned in public when he defended the treaty. Mobs battled over it. The country was in an extremely fragile place by the summer of 1795—and then matters got worse. Washington was summoned from Mount Vernon back to Philadelphia by his secretary of war, Timothy Pickering. He joined Pickering at a dinner with Jefferson's handpicked replacement as secretary of state, Edmund Randolph. (Randolph, who joined the Washington administration at its formation as the country's first attorney general, was Jefferson's third cousin. Nepotism is not a Trumpian innovation, either. Quite the contrary, it was in full bloom in the early days of the nation. Washington's nephew Bushrod, in fact, was appointed to the U.S. Supreme Court in 1798 by John Adams.)

When Washington asked Pickering to step away from the dinner table to explain why he had asked him to return to Philadelphia, Pickering explained that the matter had to do with Randolph. "The man in the other room," he said, "is a traitor." It turned out Pickering had come into possession of some documents that indicated Randolph was having private negotiations with the French, even offering to try to tilt U.S. policy toward France in exchange for a bribe. In other words, at this moment of high crisis, it appeared that the secretary of state might himself be a spy or, at best, a man of poor judgment and questionable loyalty.

Washington considered his options and decided that a potential scandal would blow up talks concerning the Jay Treaty (to be known formally as the Treaty of Amity, Commerce and Navigation, Between His Britannic Majesty and the United States of America) and so he would sign that first and then confront Randolph. That is precisely what he did, having Randolph convey the signed treaty to the British. When subsequently confronted with the accusation of disloyalty, Randolph, outraged, stormed away from Washington's residence. In keeping with the spirit of the politics of the time, he then tried to attack Washington, even accusing him of senility. He said that Washington had a small mind and was prone to prejudice and that the approval of the Jay Treaty was simply a partisan act designed to help strengthen the Federalists.

The fight over the treaty dragged on for another year, into Washington's last year in office, 1796. The House needed to appropriate $90,000 needed to implement the treaty. It sought to block the funding. It demanded that the president release all documents pertaining to the negotiation of the treaty. And, in yet another move that will seem eerily familiar to observers of modern politics, Washington claimed he was under no obligation to provide the documents requested. He went further, saying that the only way the House could get access to all the documents they requested would be to impeach him (something that Jefferson himself had suggested might be called for as a consequence of the perceived wrong associated in his mind with the treaty).

In the end, it did not come to that, of course. Skillful parliamentarians convinced the House that such a challenge to the president and such a failure to keep the young country's word internationally would be too damaging. The treaty was implemented, and in retrospect it is seen as having been a wise example of statecraft, avoiding a conflict that the country could ill afford and thus allowing it to gain in strength (which it did until it could yet again defeat the British during the War of 1812, ending conflict between the two countries once and for all—or at least until Donald Trump's 2019 trip to a London where streets were clogged with protestors, over which were floating inflatable Trump-baby blimps.)

As for internal battles, like those between Hamilton and Jefferson and the parties they headed, those grew even more acid. Washington stopped speaking to Jefferson, and the two were estranged by the time of his death in December 1799. His successor, John Adams, had such a chilly relationship with Vice President Jefferson that he did not attend Jefferson's inauguration, making him the first of only four presidents to decline to be present when his successor was sworn in. (The next would be Adams's son John Quincy Adams, as it happened, who refused to attend the inauguration of Andrew Jackson.)

THE CHARACTER OF AN HONEST MAN

Change the names, and the stories of the nation's founding ring uncomfortably familiar to those we hear daily. This is disappointing perhaps. But a phenomenon of history is that as time strips away memory, it helps us forget the idiosyncracies and flaws of those who shaped events until what we are left with are (often too-good-to-be-true) heroes who can inspire us. But it is also helpful. It allows us to put into perspective our own moment, to understand what is commonplace in the public life of our country and what is egregious, what begets infamy and what earns our gratitude.

You might look back at all this and take comfort. You might say to yourself, "They were as bad as our guys are. That Jefferson was a jerk, just like all of our jerks today. There was a ton of impeachment talk way back then and corruption and partisan gridlock and even top officials who were secretly playing for other countries. There were sex scandals and journalists that were owned by the politicians. There was nepotism and hatefulness, and society was so torn apart the country very nearly failed. Whew. What a relief." Or you might be a Jeffersonian and say, "That Hamilton was a jerk, and all those Federalists remind me of the rich Eastern elites of today." You get the idea. But I would argue either approach represents the wrong takeaway.

While there is something reassuring about knowing that what seems extraordinary and therefore dangerous in our day and age is not, it is hardly the cue to say, "Nothing to see here; I can go back to my beer and my basketball game." In the first instance, we should have learned from what nearly destroyed our country at its birth and taken steps to try to avoid it. From another perspective, we should recognize that if threats to our stability and our system have always been with us, then we must be more vigilant against them than we have been. We must be more ready to react and nip them in the bud when they arise. We must be on our guard against the tendencies in our leaders and our institutions that create the conditions for such problems to bedevil us and put our ways of life at risk.

Much of what we see today surprises us. It should not. But by the same token, much of what has happened in the past should have taught us important lessons. And that, too, has not happened.

Further, if you draw the conclusion that because some of what is happening is the same so our circumstances are identical and there is little to worry about because we survived it once before, well, then, you could not be more wrong. The circumstances are not identical. The United States was a fledgling country. It is not now. Its citizens did not have precedent to draw on and protect themselves. We do. We have seen what happens when partisan differences produce inaction and let great problems fester. The tension in the earliest days between the industrial North and the agrarian South tormented America for one hundred years and resulted in the bloodiest war the world had ever seen up to that point. It very nearly destroyed America. To the extent those divisions or others like them linger, we must recognize their potential for damage.

And Donald Trump is not George Washington. Mitch McConnell is not Thomas Jefferson. Neither Nancy Pelosi nor Barack Obama are Alexander Hamilton or John Adams.

One of the reasons we did not succumb to what went wrong in the first years of our new constitutional Republic was that the men in charge, for all their flaws, also contained greatness. Jefferson wrote the Declaration of Independence. He was motivated by a powerful belief in the enlightenment idea of the inalienable rights of men. He was one of the great political philosophers in the history of the world. So, too, was Hamilton. So, too, was Madison. They could be petty. They could play hardball. But they were motivated at least in part at all times and to a much greater extent when it really counted by doing what was right. Jefferson was a slave owner who ultimately freed his slaves, a political infighter who as president doubled the size of the country and opened up its future as a continental power. Hamilton created sound money and laid the groundwork of an industrial era economy. He worked with Madison and Jay to write the Federalist Papers and to help create an operating manual for the Constitution. They fought. They even tried to destroy each other. But when push came to shove, they and those around them moved us forward, strengthened us, and they were guided by some higher sense of duty and responsibility to posterity.

Tell me that our current leaders are cut from the same cloth.

My office is in Alexandria, Virginia, Washington's hometown. You can't walk a block without encountering his presence. That's literally true in the case of my office. One block away is where Washington's "in-town" residence was. It is a humble place. It does not even have a kitchen. Washington would eat at the tavern a block or two away when he stayed there.

Another block away, a block closer to the Potomac and the capital city, which is named after our first president, there is a plaque on a building that once housed one of those taverns. It says that it was on that spot that Washington, having been elected the first president of the United States, bade farewell to his neighbors as he set out to New York to be sworn in.

I walked by that house on the morning Donald Trump was inaugurated and I stopped and reread that plaque. It was cool and still. Many of the houses seemed to date from the time Washington lived. It was easy to feel his presence. And it was chilling to think that a man like Donald Trump was assuming the office George Washington once held.

It was not just that Trump had no experience in government or in public service or even in leading a large complex organization. It was that nothing in his life revealed a shred of character that might suggest he was capable of or fit for the job. In his past were scandals and bankruptcies and allegations of fraud, hobnobbing with gangsters, and, we already knew, welcoming the assistance of a foreign enemy in winning the presidency of the United States. It is not only that he was without qualifications or character. It is that he was defective, as we would soon see, the most corrupt man ever to occupy the highest office in this country.

That, of course, is the greatest distinction between this first chapter in American history and this most recent one. George Washington was a great man who had led America in defeat and in victory. He was always praised for his great personal courage, for his dignity, and for his humility. Abigail Adams said he blended "Dignity with ease . . . the Gentleman and Soldier look agreeably blended in him." Jefferson, with whom we know he fought, commented, "He was incapable of fear, meeting personal dangers with the calmest unconcern" and begged him to remain in office after his first term was done because he felt only Washington could "hold the North and South together."

Even if he was not as Parson Weems wrote in his effusive biography of him "just as Aristides, temperate as Epictetus, patriotic as Regulus, modest as Scipio, prudent as Fabius, rapid as Marcellus, undaunted as Hannibal, as Cincinnatus disinterested, to liberty firm as Cato, as respectful of the laws as Socrates," he was a man of extraordinary character. He understood that he would be closely observed and cared about it in a way that our current "narcissist in chief" would profoundly misunderstand. Washington felt his behavior, his probity, mattered because he was under such close scrutiny. Shortly after he became president, he wrote, "I walk on untrodden ground. There is scarcely any part of my conduct [which] may not hereafter be drawn into precedent."

This awareness and a profoundly genuine sense of humility, of the costs of the freedom America had won and of the reasons that we fought, led him to a series of acts of personal choice that literally changed the world. When offered the ability to assume the title of king after the conclusion of the war, he turned it down, firmly noting that that was precisely what the colonists had risked so much to fight against. And when he concluded two terms of office, he did what Cincinnatus had done, he returned to his farm, peacefully and gratefully handing the reins of power to another.

These were great acts, establishing in the eyes of all the world not just that Washington was an extraordinary man but that America would be an extraordinary country. Even in the face of the conflicts briefly described in this chapter, the one constant was that he faced up to the challenges, managed them, made the right choices, and assumed responsibility for the errors that occurred.

That, of course, is the greatest of all differences between our time and those first years. Then, our president was one of the great men of history, renowned for his character. Today, our problems flow from a president who is one of the worst public officials in our history. Washington was threatened with impeachment because he did what was right. That is not the case with Trump. Washington faced betrayals and disloyalty within his cabinet. Trump is the source of the betrayal we face today. Washington mediated the conflicts of his era. Trump fans divisions because, like most small leaders, he seeks to bring down and divide all those around him. Washington stood up for principle. Trump stands up for Trump. Washington understood the power of humility, the importance of appearances, the value of a man's word, and enduring consequences of precedence. Trump understands none of this. He is the spoiled product of his era and his background. He has been handed all he could want from life and then some, and he has never given a moment's thought to what it cost to establish or preserve a nation, lead a government, or stand up for a single principle.

Noting such distinctions is the most important value that can come of comparing the current moment to history. Because it says, while we may have faced crises and misdeeds and even high crimes and misdemeanors, as well as treason and traitors in our past, this time it is different—and not in a good way.

In the chapters that follow we will examine each area of our current crisis in the light of past experiences that can help illuminate them and put them in perspective—from selling out the country to a foreign power to obstruction of justice, from corruption to assaulting the rule of law. By the end of the book, it is my hope that we can not only understand why today's situation is different but why it is more dangerous than perhaps any other we have faced, other than the Civil War, and what, if anything, history suggests we can do about it.

2

AID AND COMFORT

There is nothing that keeps wicked Men at any one Moment,
out of Hell, but the mere Pleasure of GOD.

—Jonathan Edwards, "Sinners in the Hands of an Angry God"

When I was a small boy, my family drove from our home in Berkeley Heights, New Jersey, about an hour south to Princeton. My father, a scientist and teacher, was giving a lecture there. My mother, seeking to find a way to keep her two small sons occupied, took us to a cemetery.

As strange a choice as it was for diverting two little boys, in retrospect, it was stranger still. My mother brought us to see a particular hero of hers. I remember approaching the gravestone. It stood taller than I was at the time, or so it seemed to me. The stone was weathered, white-gray in the front, blackened on the sides. Behind it lay a row of aboveground crypts. The stone read:

AARON BURR
Born Feb 6th, 1756
Died Sept 14th, 1836

A Colonel in the Army of the Revolution.
Vice President of the United States from 1801 to 1805.

I remember my mom explaining to us that she had always had a soft spot in her heart for Burr. She was raised in Manhattan. He had made much of his career there despite being born in New Jersey, the son of a minister who was one of the founders of Princeton and the grandson of perhaps America's most famous early theologian, Jonathan Edwards. He entered what we know today as Princeton University when he was thirteen and studied theology himself. I remember she said he had once been in a duel with a man named Alexander Hamilton and that he had killed him. I thought it odd that she admired someone who had killed a man, but she explained that Burr had not gotten a fair shake from history and that Hamilton was not a good guy, either.

It would take much of my life to fill in all the gaps of the story, and today, many biographies and one prominent Broadway musical later, I would still wager most people do not really understand just how wrong my mother was. Burr was literally a man who could, as President Trump has fantasized, shoot a man not too far from where Fifth Avenue is today and get away with it—and he was actually vice president of the United States at the time he did just that. But, more strikingly, it was not the worst thing Burr did in public life. The worst thing he did led to him becoming the highest-level U.S. official tried for treason in our history, in a case that would set important precedents for how we look at betrayals like those of Donald Trump, just over two centuries later.

It is not that Hamilton was exactly a knight on a white horse, either. He was ambitious, combative, scheming, and a philanderer. But he was also one of the handful of men whose genius helped ensure that the American experiment would survive its infancy. Burr, to the contrary, seemed to do his best to undo or threaten that experiment, mostly by placing its fate second to his own personal ambitions, and his betrayals and bad judgments have echoed through time until the present, rivaled only by those of the fathers of the Southern rebellion that triggered the Civil War, as among the worst in our history. Today, of course, it is a list that includes near its top another supremely self-interested, ambitious, philandering, untrustworthy New Yorker, the forty-fifth president of the United States.

While Burr's early entry into Princeton was a sign of his promise, it was a consequence of getting into college the old-fashioned way: via connections. Of course, unlike Trump's connections, which were simply those associated with money—the best avenue available to recent immigrant families—Burr's were of a different sort, more essential in the eighteenth century: being born into the right sort of family. While Burr's mother was the daughter of one of the most prominent theologians in the United States, one of the architects for a religious movement called the First Great Awakening, a reaction against more-tolerant religious practices in England's American colonies, his father was the son of a wealthy landowner in Connecticut who was caught up in that movement, which is how he came to meet Burr's mother.

Burr's father, Aaron Sr., who studied at Yale (which happened to be founded by a group that included his mother-in-law's father) became a clergyman himself and an academic, moving to the state of New Jersey where he—along with Edwards and others—helped to found the College of New Jersey (now Princeton), in part out of a reaction that took place at Yale against core ideas of the Great Awakening. When the first president of the university died, two years after its founding in 1746, Burr Sr. became president at age thirty-two. To this day he is the second-youngest person ever to be president of the university. During his tenure he moved the university from Newark, New Jersey, to its current home, Princeton, and supervised the construction of its first building there, today known as Nassau Hall. Aaron Burr, Jr., was born in 1756, the year the college moved to Princeton. Sadly, his father would die the next year, and his mother in 1758.

Burr and his infant sister, now orphans, were placed in the custody of another family associated with the founding of Princeton, that of William Shippen of Philadelphia. Remember the name. Even though the Burr children were with the Shippens for just one year until a maternal uncle could come of age and assume their care, the name Shippen will return as part of our brief look at the history of traitors and treason in America. Because Shippen's brother, Edward, would later have a granddaughter named Peggy, who at the age of eighteen would become the wife and a great (and dangerous) influence in the life of someone with whom Burr was himself to become associated—first as a soldier and later in the annals of American treason—Benedict Arnold.

POSTERITY'S COURT

Young Aaron Burr was unhappy being raised by his young uncle Timothy Edwards and tried to run away several times. Thus, when at the age of thirteen he went off to Princeton, he was delighted to be on his own. He studied theology and then, at the age of nineteen, chose to shift his focus to the study of law. Fortunately, his sister had married a man named Tapping Reeve, who happened to have founded America's first law school in

Litchfield, Connecticut. In 1775, while Aaron was studying there, news reached the school of the battles of Lexington and Concord, and Burr, looking to establish a name for himself, decided to enlist in the Continental Army.

The first major campaign in which Burr was involved was, in fact, led by a group of senior officers that included Benedict Arnold, then a colonel in his mid-thirties, who had come from a good family that had seen some hard times and who wanted to restore his standing. Colonel Arnold led an overland expedition to Quebec City through the backwoods of Maine, one that was so grueling for his troops that almost half of the eleven hundred men under his command turned back or died. And although ultimately, in the Battle of Montreal, the colonists lost to the British forces, both Arnold and the much more junior Burr acquitted themselves bravely. Another officer in this campaign, whose life would intersect with Burr's for years and ultimately bring disgrace to both men, was a young captain named James Wilkinson. If Arnold is America's most famous traitor, it is only because people have forgotten Wilkinson, who was every bit as treacherous—or worse.

Each of these men went on to greater responsibility as a result of their early successes during the revolution. Arnold, for his heroism, became a favorite of General George Washington. The other two, Burr and Wilkinson, never found the general's favor and, in fact, would have careers that would be colored by his enduring distrust of them and their consequent resentment of Washington. Burr, for example, after Quebec, served briefly as an adjutant to Washington, but they never clicked—unlike the young man who also joined the general's team at about the same time and became one of Washington's closest and most trusted aides: Alexander Hamilton.

Arnold, of course, went on to become the best-known traitor in American history. In a story that bears faint echoes to that of America's current president—and also to Burr and Wilkinson—Arnold was eager for social approval and position. He had a tumultuous relationship with fellow officers in the Continental Army, but his good relationship with Washington led to his being made the military governor of Philadelphia in 1778. Taking advantage of this, he did what a number of other senior officers did in those rough-and-tumble times and sought to capitalize on his position financially—participating in schemes that took advantage of his power to profit from military-supply deals. This helped support the lavish lifestyle he felt was only appropriate for a man of his stature in prospering Philadelphia. As part of the active social life he enjoyed as the top officer of the Continental Army in that city, he dined and partied with many of the city's most notable residents. In particular, he became acquainted with an eighteen-year-old beauty from a very prominent local family, the Shippens, the same family that had briefly taken in the young, orphaned Burr years before. This young woman, Peggy Shippen, was close to her father, who in turn had remained close to the British throughout the war.

Soon those who felt ill-treated by the high-handed Arnold or those who felt hard done by because of his dealings, accused him of unethical behavior. Whether it was these emerging scandals surrounding his business deals, his enduring sense of not being treated as he felt he deserved to be, or the influence of his loyalist wife, by the spring of 1779 Arnold was so disaffected that he offered his services by way of an intermediary to the British commander in New York, Sir Henry Clinton. Clinton gave permission to his handsome young spy chief, Major John André, to engage Arnold. Within months Arnold was providing the British with information about troop locations, movements, and capabilities.

Fortunately for Arnold the spy, despite having been found guilty of improper financial practices, he maintained a close relationship with Washington, who was often forced by circumstance to overlook the imperfections of some of the commanders who reported to him.

Washington was therefore open to Arnold being assigned to a different command. Specifically, the possibility arose of Arnold's being reassigned as the commander at West Point, a fort in a strategic position on the Hudson River. As this possibility grew more likely, Arnold let his British counterparts know that he might be in a position to provide them with valuable information regarding the fort that might even enable them to "take it without loss." What he wanted in exchange for the information was money, more money than he had already received.

By August 1780, Arnold had not only won the West Point assignment but he received an offer of twenty thousand pounds from the British, delivered to him by his wife, Peggy. He accepted the terms and proposed a meeting with André. He did so by passing on a coded letter through an intermediary. Arnold provided the plans of the fort to André as well as passes so that André could move freely behind American lines.

André's capture in late September by three local New York militiamen marked the unraveling of the plans. Arnold immediately made his way to New York and there requested that, despite everything, Washington grant his wife safe passage to meet him. Washington again acceded. André was hanged within days. (It should be noted that, to illustrate again what a small world America was in those days, a plea was made for mercy for André by a young woman who had met him once at her father's home and found him charming. The woman was Eliza Schuyler, daughter of the general who had commanded the Quebec campaign and who was soon to be the wife of Alexander Hamilton.)

Arnold, however, escaped and took up a role as a brigadier general in the British Army. He led a number of operations against the Americans, several quite successful. Shortly afterward he went to England seeking to win the favor of senior officials, but there were many who distrusted him and saw him only as an opportunist who betrayed his fellow colonists for money. His wife joined him in England, and later they sought to do business in Saint John, New Brunswick, but were not terribly successful. He then returned for the last years of life to England, which never fully accepted him, but where he managed to live in comfort until his death in 1801.

History has not, for obvious reasons, been kind to America's most prominent early traitor. Washington ultimately was deeply embittered by the betrayal of a man he so trusted and to whom he had extended so many favors and courtesies. Benjamin Franklin wrote, "Judas sold only one man, Arnold three millions." History after history has made his name synonymous with selling out the United States and aiding our enemies. Yet today, as we look back at what he did, as clear as his crimes were, he did not—try as he might—in the end do any material damage to the U.S. cause during the revolution. Indeed, perhaps that is why greater subsequent betrayals by even-higher-level officials were ultimately viewed as more serious. For example, at the outset of the Civil War, *Harper's Weekly* described Jefferson Davis and the other headmen of the Confederacy as guilty of a "colossal treason, by whose side Benedict Arnold shines white as a saint."

The questions we might ask as we compare Arnold and subsequent traitors and other manner of betrayers of the United States are: What was the nature of the trust and role given to the individual or individuals involved? What was the context of their actions? And what were the consequences of those actions? Without seeking to exculpate Arnold in the slightest, it must be noted that while he was a general, he was already viewed with distrust and skepticism by others in top positions in the Continental Army, and so his access to information and influence was rather limited. Further, he made the decision to switch sides surrounded by a community in Philadelphia and throughout the colonies that included many loyalists. Indeed, it is worth remembering that he was born a British subject and that, of course, the view of most of the world was that it was the American revolutionaries who were illegally at war with their recognized sovereign. In other words, it was a period of flux in which loyalties naturally were pulled in multiple directions. Finally, the consequences of his actions were, in the end, worse for the British—who lost their spy chief André and who saw public opinion galvanized against them by nature of Arnold's treachery—than they were for the Americans.

In short, Arnold was a nasty piece of work, no doubt about it, and he has earned his special place among the villains of American history. But in terms of damage he actually inflicted, the impact was not on a par with that of the leaders of the Confederacy—nor, in fact, with that done by someone who encouraged the illicit help of a foreign enemy to win the presidency and then used that position to reward that enemy, weaken our alliances, damage our standing, irreparably despoil our environment, undercut our institutions, and do irreparable harm to minorities, immigrants, the poor, and those whose political views or political leaders he may have opposed.

That said, consider the consequences of Arnold's betrayal. Consider history's judgment. Arnold was not tried nor was he punished. In fact, he was rewarded for his crimes and got away with them. Yet time has imposed the ultimate sentence on him—ignominy and everlasting shame. His name his come to be synonymous with betraying the country. For Donald Trump and those close to him who feel that avoiding near-term consequences is tantamount to victory, this and the story of the others who have sold out the country make it clear that time and time again, posterity strips away technicalities and zeroes in on the core truth of bad acts.

As we shall see, in fact, with a few notable exceptions we'll review, almost all of those who committed the most traitorous acts against the United States escaped the most severe legal consequences, leaving the harshest judgment to be made by posterity's court.

THE UNCERTAIN LOYALTIES OF AN ERA OF REBELLION

In the early days of the new Republic, the turmoil of the establishment of the new nation and the fluid sense of loyalties and institutions in the wake of a revolution, as well as the still-uncertain relationship between individual states and the federal government, produced instances in which authorities actually did seek to affirm the authority of the new government by charging those who ignored its power with treason.

The first of these instances illustrated well the fact that America was still getting its sea legs as a society. Shortly after the ratification of the Constitution and the establishment of the new government, Secretary of the Treasury Alexander Hamilton sought to help shore up the United States' financial situation by levying taxes. This was not a power afforded the federal government under the short-lived government created immediately after the revolution under the terms of the Articles of Confederation, and some saw it as an effort to overempower the now constitutionally empowered federal government to the detriment of the power that they felt ought to be afforded to the states. The first tax imposed on any domestically produced product was levied on whiskey. Across the country, howls of complaint were heard, especially in rural areas on the more lawless fringes of the new Republic, such as western Pennsylvania.

Those protesting the tax used heavy-handed means to keep the federal government from collecting it. Hundreds of armed men sought to intimidate the tax collectors, and President Washington called for troops from local militias to put down the uprising. Small confrontations were interspersed with efforts to negotiate, as Washington was seeking to strike a balance between confirming the federal government's power and not tearing the fledgling country apart at the same time. (It is worth noting here that one member of the cabinet, Alexander Hamilton, the architect of the taxes, took to writing under a pen name in Philadelphia newspapers, asserting that part of the cause of the violence was the agitation of Democratic-Republican Societies, in other words, supporters of the party of his rivals Jefferson and Burr.) Ultimately, the crisis was resolved when Washington himself, with Hamilton at his side, rode out at the head of a unit of the country's small standing army to confront the rebels, and resistance collapsed.

Many rebels fled. But up to twenty-four were indicted for treason. Of those, only two were convicted—Philip Vigol and John Mitchell. Vigol had been guilty of burning a tax collector's house, while Mitchell, whom history records as being rather dim-witted, actually did very little indeed and may in fact have been duped into action. Washington pardoned both, and while his handling of the situation won widespread approval, the divide over the power of the federal government ultimately fueled the victory of Jefferson and Burr over Washington's handpicked successor, John Adams, in 1800.

Adams, too, had faced a similar problem when he sought to levy a tax to help pay for the so-called Quasi-War with France, an undeclared conflict that nonetheless was beyond the means of the tiny government. Once again, in the wilds of frontier Pennsylvania, resistance to the tax spread and small groups of rebels resisted paying taxes. Adams called out troops, and the tax resisters were rounded up, including their leader, John Fries. Thirty men were tried, and Fries and two others were brought up on treason charges. Once again, Adams, like Washington, pardoned them—citing the narrowness of the constitutional definition of treason, which we discussed earlier.

These cases, covered here because the term "treason" was used, hardly rise to the level of what we consider treason today. But the term arose because of the resistance of the agitators to the federal government, their unwillingness to be bound by federal laws, and the threat that posed to the rule of law in the United States, something that does indeed resonate two centuries later and has often come up during the intervening centuries.

Burr became vice president in 1800 via the rather tortured process imposed upon voters by the Electoral College. Back then, both candidates on a party's ticket each ran for president and then the top two vote-getters in the Electoral College would become president and vice president. Jefferson and Burr ended up being tied (after Burr had politicked his way up from fourth place) at seventy-three votes each, and the vote went to the House of Representatives. After thirty-five ballots the two were still tied. Then, even though he saw Jefferson as his foremost rival, none other than Alexander Hamilton—the former Treasury secretary and subsequently the top officer in the U.S. military—worked behind the scenes to ensure Burr did not prevail, because he saw Burr as dangerous, a man of questionable character. He engineered several Federalists to vote for Jefferson, thus ensuring he would become the third president of the United States.

After the election, Hamilton returned to private life in New York while Vice President Burr, also deeply distrusted by Jefferson (following the election shenanigans), was iced out of any significant role in the Jefferson administration. By 1804, Burr's character was as plain to Jefferson as it was to Hamilton, and he was dropped from the ticket. As John Sedgwick, author of a history of the relationship between Hamilton and Burr, described the man who was clearly the lesser of the two, "There is such a thing as Hamiltonianism, there's Jeffersonianism. There isn't Burrism. Burr was not an ideologist. He was a total opportunist, who would go whichever way proved the greatest advantage to him."

That perspective was anathema to Hamilton, and when Burr decided that he would run for governor of New York, it was none other than Hamilton who again worked tirelessly behind the scenes to engineer his fellow New Yorker's defeat. He called Burr the "Catiline of America," a reference to the Roman whom Cicero decried as a traitor and a villain.

When Burr got wind of Hamilton's attacks on him, he demanded an apology. Hamilton refused, and the duel they fought on the heights of Weehawken across the Hudson River from New York on July 11, 1804, was the result. It is said Hamilton fired into the air (the term for this was "throwing away" his shot, which a couple hundred years later led to a key refrain in the musical based on Hamilton's life). Whatever the case, thirty-six hours after being struck by a ball fired from Burr's pistol, Hamilton was dead and Burr was the subject of massive public condemnation. Indeed, the former senator and vice president who had hoped to be New York's governor was forced to flee the state to avoid prosecution. He made his way via Philadelphia to South Carolina, to the home of his married daughter, Theodosia.

From there, he sought to regain his footing and to find a way to have his stature restored. He finished out his term as vice president, careful to avoid jurisdictions where overzealous law-enforcement officers might arrest him for his murder of Hamilton. Although not well known as an orator, he finished his time as vice president with a speech before the Senate in which he offered words that resonate today. He said, "This house is a sanctuary, a citadel of law, of order, and of liberty; it is here—it is here, in this exalted refuge; here, if anywhere, will resistance be made to the storms of political phrenzy and the silent arts of corruption; and if the Constitution be destined ever to perish by the sacrilegious hands of the demagogue or the usurper, which God avert, its expiring agonies will be witnessed on this floor." Reportedly senators wept when he concluded, but there were more tears to come.

Burr's circuitous path ultimately took him westward. There, he entered into a convoluted series of plans that reflected and sought to tap into the dark side of the enterprising spirit of the revolutionaries who founded the United States. Like the farmers who rose up against the United States in the Whiskey Rebellion and in Fries's uprising shortly after, many of those who had gone west in the United States had done so to be free of society's fetters and to draft their own narratives, much as the "fathers" of the new nation had proven could be done just years earlier.

Burr fell in with a group who sought, according to later testimony by witnesses, to seize lands that were owned by Spain and Mexico in Louisiana and Texas. Unfortunately for Burr, one of those he invited to join his plans was his old Revolutionary War friend James Wilkinson, now General James Wilkinson—a man who had also come to be known by then to many schemes and plots, from one to separate Kentucky from Virginia, to his own independent negotiations, which continued over a period of years, to work with the Spanish to pare off bits of the United States and put them under Spanish control. Nonetheless, despite the fact that few trusted Wilkinson, including those who colluded with him, he had risen to follow in the footsteps of both Washington and Hamilton as the most senior general in the U.S. Army.

Washington and Hamilton had both viewed him as profoundly unreliable but kept him on by dangling future advancement as a possibility. Becoming senior general of the army was his reward. (That said, the hope and expectation was that there would be little use for this army beyond keeping the peace.) Jefferson trusted Wilkinson more than Washington and made him one of two men with the responsibility for overseeing the takeover of the Louisiana Territory from the French. He was based in New Orleans, where again he made himself open to the highest bidder, actually, as was later revealed, by cashing in a bribe received from the Spanish government for information and assistance with their concerns about the future of the Florida territories they controlled.

Burr and Wilkinson reconnected, and the two further

developed plans to create an "Empire of the West." Burr had initially sought British aid for the scheme, but it did not materialize. Subsequently he had raised some money for the plan from a rich Irish immigrant named Harman Blennerhassett—using the money to purchase some lands that could provide a staging area for his scheme. He recruited a small following of westerners while making his way along the Mississippi to New Orleans. This stirred again long-bubbling suspicions in Washington, D.C., and Wilkinson, it seems, was spooked by these rumblings. So, while telling Burr he was working with him, he quietly blew the whistle on him, sending a letter describing the Burr plan and the risks it posed to the country to authorities late in the fall of 1806.

Central to his accusations were the contents of a cipher letter reportedly describing the Burr plan. The letter itself, when examined closely at trial, appeared tampered with, some suspect by Wilkinson to protect himself or make him look better. But the core of its content proved damning. In it, Burr describes his plan:

> "I, Aaron Burr, have obtained funds and have actually commenced the enterprise. Detachments from different points and under different pretenses, will rendezvous on the Ohio 1st November. . . . Protection of England is secured. Truxtun is going to Jamaica to arrange with the [British] admiral on that station, and will meet at the Mississippi—England—a navy of the United States, are ready to join, and final orders are given to my friends and followers. It will be a host of choice spirits. Wilkinson shall be second to Burr only. . . . Burr will proceed westward 1st August, never to return: with him goes his daughter; the husband will follow in October,

with a corps of worthies. . . . The project is brought to the
point so long desired. Burr guarantees the result with his
life and honor—the lives and honor and the fortunes of hun-
dreds, the best blood of our country. Burr's plan of operation
is to move down rapidly from the Falls [of the Ohio] on the
15th of November, with the first five hundred or one thou-
sand men, in light boats now constructing for that purpose;
to be at Natchez between the 5th and 15th of December, there
to meet you; there to determine whether it will be expedient,
in the first instance, to seize or pass by Baton Rouge. . . . The
gods invite us to glory and fortune."

So as Burr proceeded with his plot and rumors of it spread, word of his treachery also began to make its way to official circles. While men like Andrew Jackson celebrated Burr with fancy balls and welcomed him as a guest in their homes (Jackson scoffed at the unfair treatment Burr had following his duel, given Jackson's familiarity and comfort with resolving differences "on the field of honor"), others began to take action.

The U.S. district attorney, a brother-in-law of U.S. Supreme Court Chief Justice Marshall, Joseph Daveiss, had been warning Jefferson of the perils on the frontier for months—citing his concerns about both Burr and Wilkinson. On November 8, 1806, he presented an affidavit in federal court charging Burr and an associate of illegally planning an attack against Mexico. As it happened, the judge was himself accused of being too close to Spain and the case was thwarted. Burr sought to clear his name, and with that in mind, he hired a local lawyer named Henry Clay to represent him. Clay was momentarily successful in defending Burr's honor—an early step on his path to become Speaker of the U.S. House of Representatives and U.S. secretary of state.

But Jefferson had become persuaded of the risk posed by Burr, and he was incensed that he seemed to be escaping legal consequences for his plotting and scheming. As a consequence, by way of seeking to tighten the noose around his former vice president, Jefferson issued a proclamation stating that "sundry persons . . . are conspiring and confederating together to begin . . . a military expedition or enterprise against the dominions of Spain" and requiring that "all faithful citizens who have been led without due knowledge or consideration to participate in the said unlawful enterprises to withdraw from same without delay."

For a while, Burr continued to dodge prosecution and enjoy the hospitality of the South. But ultimately, prodded by the Virginian in the White House, the federal vise tightened around him, and he was apprehended while trying to disappear into the countryside in disguise.

The case consumed Jefferson. He already had come to dislike Burr, and in an extraordinary move for a sitting president, declared him guilty of treason even prior to his trial. The Congress—including many members critical of the president for getting so deeply involved in a judicial matter—demanded evidence of crimes, and Jefferson, though angered by their demands, accommodated them, asserting at the time that Burr was an "archconspirator" and that his guilt was beyond question.

Jefferson saw pursuing the case as a top priority and even had Secretary of State James Madison—the principal author of the Constitution—play a role not envisioned in that document by interrogating coconspirators. In the course of those negotiations, Madison even promised not to use evidence that their confessions might bring against them and then later reneged on that promise. So much for the high-minded principles of the founders.

Ultimately, the case came before the chief justice of the U.S. Supreme Court, John Marshall, a distant cousin of Jefferson's—but not by any means a political ally. In fact, the two were known to be rivals, hostile to each other for many years. Marshall inflamed Jefferson by saying that the coconspirators could not be tried in Washington, D.C., because their crimes took place elsewhere. They were released. Burr, however, when captured, was brought to Virginia, which still had jurisdiction over the area in which Burr met with Blennerhassett.

Jefferson sought in every way he knew to put his thumb on the scales of justice—in ways that may even echo events we've witnessed recently. Jefferson wanted a jury drawn exclusively from his political party. He offered to pay witnesses for their time. He provided prosecutors with blank pardons that could be used if they might induce Burr's coconspirators to testify against him. He even supported declaring martial law in New Orleans so that evidence and witnesses could be seized without warrants. He wrote that the facts published in newspapers had led to the "universal belief or rumor of [Burr's] guilt." (This was despite Jefferson's almost Trumpian view in the face of his own criticism by newspaper writers, deeply ironic for a champion of a free press, that "Nothing can now be believed which is in a newspaper. I will add, that the man who never looks into a newspaper is better informed than he who reads them; inasmuch as he who knows nothing is nearer to truth than he whose mind is filled with falsehoods and errors." Shades of "fake news"!)

While Jefferson had prepared his own account of Burr's actions, which he provided to Congress, Marshall required

Jefferson to present it himself in front of the Court. Jefferson refused to do so, asserting that the judiciary did not have the power to compel such behavior by a president. Then, as the 140 witnesses for the prosecution began their testimony, it became clear that most were dealing in rumors and hearsay.

Burr's lawyers, including one Edmund Randolph—the man who had succeeded Jefferson as secretary of state, yet another of Jefferson's cousins, until he was run from office by Washington for his own disloyalty and behind-the-scenes communications with the French—argued that the evidence could not support the accusation of treason. Their case rested on the fact—yet again—that the constitutional definition of "treason" is very narrow, requiring two witnesses to overt acts of "levying war" against the United States or in "giving . . . Aid and Comfort" or "adhering" to a foreign enemy. Marshall ruled that the case against Burr did not meet that standard—which both set Burr free and set an important precedent for recognizing extremely high standards required for treason convictions in the United States. He specifically focused on the fact that the accused must be seen to participate in a treasonable act. Burr had not, in his view, been seen to do so. Marshall, in his decision, wrote, "It is, then, the opinion of the court that this indictment can be supported only by testimony which proves the accused to have been actually or constructively present when the assemblage [of those engaging in the treasonable act] took place." He found that no witness could place Burr in such a setting. (The roots of the narrow provisions are in English law dating back to the year 1350—although back then treason also included "imagining" the death of the king as well as counterfeiting money, killing high officials, and having sexual relations with certain women in the royal court. Given the state of politics in America today, it is a good thing they did not retain as a crime the imagining of something awful befalling the head of state. Had they kept that law in place, judging from my Twitter feed alone, thousands of Americans would be arrested daily.)

Jefferson was outraged and later contemplated how presidents might be able, with the cooperation of Congress, to remove judges from office—an idea that fortunately, short of impeachment, did not become law. Burr was nonetheless disgraced and lived out the remainder of his days unable to clear himself despite repeated efforts to do so. The story of his last years is sordid and involves unsuccessful scheming to make ends meet, prostitutes, opium, and social intrigues. He died in New York in 1836.

Wilkinson was promoted for his "efforts," but his character did not change. He was court-martialed for corruption in 1811, though he escaped conviction. He was unsuccessful on the battlefield in the War of 1812, and then after he renewed his ties with the Spanish, once again trying to enrich himself by working on their behalf. He died in Mexico City in 1825.

In retrospect, Wilkinson was undoubtedly a more committed traitor than even Burr. From his participation in the so-called Conway Cabal, which sought to remove Washington as general of the Continental Army, to years of cashing in on relationships with the Spanish, he was as close to a lifelong career traitor as the United States has ever produced. The jury foreman in the Burr trial characterized Wilkinson as "a mammoth of iniquity . . . The only man that I ever saw who was from the bark to the very core a villain." Later, one historian, Frederick Turner, went even further, describing him as he certainly was, as "The most consummate artist in treason the nation has ever possessed."

Looking back over 240 years of American history, the cases of Burr and Wilkinson stand out for several reasons. First, Burr is the highest-ranking U.S. government official until Trump to have been credibly accused of betraying the country. He is the highest-ranking U.S. official ever to have actually been legally accused of treason. And the plots of Burr and Wilkinson—to actually break up the United States—were the most serious high-level such efforts until the Civil War, when the Confederacy was also led by a man who, like Burr, was a former senator and later a top official in a presidential administration, Jefferson Davis, who had served as secretary of war in the cabinet of President Franklin Pierce.

Having said all that, Burr's plot did not advance very far, nor did Wilkinson's various efforts on behalf of the Spanish or himself. Burr allegedly reached out to the British for assistance, and Wilkinson to the Spanish—both rivals of the United States—but the British demurred and the Spanish primarily sought information regarding the protection of their own lands. There is no evidence they sought to break up the United States. Neither attacked nor weakened American institutions, gave material advantage to foreign adversaries, nor did either employ the power of high office to advance their betrayals or ensure justice was not done. As a consequence, their acts of betrayal are, as were Benedict Arnold's, different in consequence, character, and, indeed, odiousness from those of candidate and then President Trump, based on the facts as we know them from Special Counsel Robert Mueller's report (*Report on the Investigation into Russian Interference in the 2016 Presidential Election*) and other sources.

Just how stark the contrast is between Trump and past traitors is even more clearly illuminated, as we will see in the next chapter, by those who were accused of betraying the country in the midst of the great wars that threatened its existence—the Civil War, World War I, World War II, the Cold War and, most recently, the "War on Terror." We will examine those instances and then compare them to what we know about the actions of Trump from the Mueller Report, the congressional investigation into the Ukraine case and other legal cases, and the public record.

3

THE WARS WITHIN

I am worth inconceivably more to hang than for any other purpose.

—John Brown

A HOUSE DIVIDED

Months after Burr was hustled before courts in Kentucky, a boy was born a few hundred miles away, in the western part of the state. The year after, another boy was born, also in Kentucky, as legend and fact would have it, in a log cabin. The first would oversee the greatest threat to the survival of the United States ever and the greatest act of treason in our history. The second would crush that threat and then signal his desire not to punish the wrongdoers too severely before he himself was assassinated.

Jefferson Davis was born in what is now Fairview, Kentucky, in June 1808. Abraham Lincoln was born just over one hundred miles away and eight months later in Hodgenville. But the tensions that ultimately led to their being the leaders on opposite sides in the bloodiest conflict the world had known until that time were born decades before, in the first moments of America, when the founders grappled with core questions like the future of slavery, states' rights, and how to integrate the goals and needs of the agrarian South and the industrializing North.

Those tensions led to the emergence of two very different schools of thought concerning what the country was to be about and to circumstances in which what one man might have claimed was patriotism was viewed by another—or by history—as traitorous betrayal.

They percolated for years beneath the surface but never disappeared. Occasionally, they would flare up. In fact, the birth of the country itself was an act of secession, and since that birth, the topic would arise again regularly for one hundred years (to say nothing of the much more remote possibility that it has arisen again recently with scattered, not terribly serious talk of California—now the world's fifth largest economy on its own—contemplating pulling away from a Trumpian America with politics very much unlike those of the Golden State).

The way the country went from its original very loose structure in the Articles of Confederation to the Constitution was due to the fact that many states simply chose not to follow the terms of those articles—because they felt the principle of states' rights was more important, more basic, than any linking the thirteen colonies. When the Constitution was drafted to address this problem, it sidestepped the idea of unanimous ratification required in the Articles of Confederation to going into effect when just nine of the thirteen colonies approved it. Once nine did, they proceeded, leaving the other four states on their own to determine whether they wished to be affiliated with the new nation or not. (North Carolina and Rhode Island did not participate in the first election under the Constitution because they had yet to make up their minds on the subject.)

Then, very early on in the life of the country, even the founders grappled with whether states had a real claim on independent jurisdiction apart from the central government, with the champion of the view that they did being—unsurprisingly—Jefferson. Indeed, Jefferson, who we earlier saw was the first senior official to attack a president for being a traitor in the case of Washington and the Jay Treaty, actually contemplated secession as a reasonable response for states that disapproved of federal laws. And he did so as vice president of the United States.

When the Federalist president under which Jefferson served as vice president, John Adams, introduced the Alien and Sedition Acts, they triggered great controversy. Once again, these laws, passed in 1798, echo discussions that would seem very familiar today. In part they made it harder for immigrants to become citizens and enabled the president to imprison and deport aliens he felt posed a threat, focusing especially on those associated with a hostile nation (a law that remains in effect today). They also made it against the law to spread false statements critical of the government.

Adams and the Federalists asserted the laws were needed to protect the country in the midst of the so-called Quasi-War with France. But Jefferson and supporters like James Madison were particularly outraged by the encroachment on freedom of speech that came as part of the Sedition Act, the one that made it a crime to spread false statements critical of the government, soon to be located in Washington, D.C., in 1800. They did not stop with criticizing the acts, however. They promoted the idea that states had the right to nullify federal laws in defense of their own independence and fundamental rights. While they hoped this would not result in fragmentation of the new union, in the summer of 1799, Jefferson wrote to Madison saying that while he hoped people would accept their views "were we to be disappointed in this," then those who agreed with them should be ready "to sever ourselves from that union we so much value, rather than give up the rights of self government."

The idea was not exclusively one embraced by southerners, either. When young John C. Calhoun attended Yale University just a couple years later, he studied with the university's president, Timothy Dwight. Dwight was perhaps a typical northern intellectual of the time and was no fan of Jefferson's views on many issues. But he did inculcate in Calhoun—later seen as the architect of the South's decades-long contemplation of the idea of seceding over the issue of slavery—the idea that secession was a legitimate option to consider, although he made the case that should the northern states not be able to resolve their differences with the South then perhaps they should be the ones to withdraw from the new and obviously very fragile country. These ideas and the embrace of Jefferson and Madison's idea of nullification were further established in his thinking when Calhoun went on to study law—at the law school of Aaron Burr's brother-in-law, Tapping Reeve, in Litchfield, Connecticut.

Calhoun's views deepened on these issues as he entered politics—first as a congressman from South Carolina in 1811, later as secretary of war for James Monroe from 1817 to 1825, and then as vice president of the United States to two of the most different men to serve as president, John Quincy Adams, whom Calhoun served from 1825 to 1829, and then his successor, Andrew Jackson, whom Calhoun served tumultuously from 1829 to 1832.

Throughout this period the nation remained in a fragile

state. When Calhoun was secretary of war, he was first introduced to Jackson as a general who led the invasion of Spanish-
controlled Florida—without any authorization from the Monroe
administration. Later, however, the first spasms of the struggle
that was to define Calhoun's life and the fate of the new nation
were manifest, when in 1818 pioneers in the Missouri Territory
sought admission to the Union as a slave state. This was not well
received in the North, and laws were proposed that would limit
the spread of slavery into Missouri should it become a state.
This sparked furious debate and, again, talk of the dissolution
of the Union.

Another issue that triggered the antipathy of states' rights
advocates in the South were high tariffs, an issue on which
Adams and Calhoun were split. Calhoun was a candidate
for president in 1824 against Adams and others, including
Jackson. While Calhoun distrusted Jackson based on his prior
experience with him, he felt he would be a relief from the Fed-
eralism of Adams and better for the states' rights cause. While
he was right about this in some areas, almost from the beginning Calhoun's relationship with Jackson was toxic, and
he was soon cut out by the president (a common fate of vice
presidents, as we have seen). Nonetheless, while in office, Calhoun used his prodigious intellectual gifts to further advance
the case for nullification as a way to maintain the goals of the
founders to counterbalance and contain a tyrannous central
government.

His views are laid out in a document he wrote called *South
Carolina Exposition and Protest*. In it he argued that states essentially had a veto power over federal decisions they deemed
contra-constitutional. His views were a clear expression of a
view that was taking hold across the South first on the issue of

tariffs but then, beyond that, on the issue of slavery. Leaving the vice presidency, Calhoun remained in the mix as a senator from South Carolina, and in this position he continued to advance the view that he would soon describe with these words: "in a contest between the State and the General Government, if the resistance be limited on both sides to the civil process, the State, by its inherent sovereignty, standing upon its reserved powers, will prove too powerful in such a controversy, and must triumph over the Federal Government."

He spoke those words on the floor of the Senate in the midst of what would be called the Nullification Crisis, when South Carolina nullified two tariffs passed by the federal government. Jackson responded by sending warships to Charleston. A desperate set of legislative negotiations began to hold the Union together—at the center of which were Calhoun's and Burr's former attorney, former Speaker of the House, Henry Clay. The crisis was defused, but even as it was, Calhoun laid down the principle described in the preceding paragraph so eloquently that it became an even more prominent factor in U.S. politics in the decades of strife to come.

THE FAILURE OF COMPROMISE

At this point, it is worth taking a moment to explain why I am going into detail explaining, for example, the history of nullification and secession. The purpose of this book, after all, is to understand how history will view Donald Trump's presidency, and to examine how his crimes and abuses may compare with those of others who betrayed the country in U.S. history. To do this, though, as I hope I have made clear along the way, it is essential that we understand the context of past betrayals. This is critical to know how to objectively evaluate where the current administration stands. But it is also important because many of our views of history are shaped by myths, faded memories, and emotions, and in the context of the values and standards of our own times.

Secession or nullification sound radical and anathema to the ideas of America that have evolved over the past 160 years. They sound especially evil when they are interpolated with the repugnant idea of slavery, which they were ultimately deployed to defend. But, as we have seen, these were views that were in the mainstream of American political discourse from before the revolution through the Civil War. Those who advocated them therefore were not viewed in their day in quite the same way as we view them today—a fact that will be clearly illustrated by the treatment of those who were complicit in the greatest, most dangerous, most costly act of betrayal in American history, the Civil War. This is not to minimize their crimes. It is simply to refine our understanding. The facts of the case explicate that further.

During the decades leading up to the war, tensions grew between pro-slavery and anti-slavery factions in the United States. Calhoun, as secretary of state under President John Tyler, presided over one such debate centering on the annexation of the state of Texas. Calhoun argued that Texas should enter the Union as a slave state and that this was in the interest of the entire nation because it would "diffuse" slavery over a broader area. The argument was unpersuasive, unsurprisingly, to anti-slavery advocates, and the first effort to admit Texas under the so-called Tyler-Texas Treaty failed. Leading to Tyler's loss in the next election, it was a central issue in the election, and after southerner James K. Polk of Tennessee won, the treaty did pass. But the issue did not go away.

THE DEBATE INTENSIFIES, AND BLOOD FLOWS

The United States acquired more of the West in the wake of the Mexican-American War, and it was clear that the debate over whether new states would be pro- or anti-slavery grew more intense. Henry Clay and a new senator, Stephen Douglas of Illinois, tried to address this in an initiative called the Compromise of 1850, which set the rules for entry into the Union for California, New Mexico, and Utah. While it postponed conflict, it only did so temporarily. Tensions grew and violence flared in the wake of the next major act to address the slavery problem, the Kansas-Nebraska Act of 1854. It allowed the people of each state to determine their own fates on the issue based on a concept dubbed "popular sovereignty." In Nebraska, there was no appetite for what Calhoun had euphemistically called the "peculiar institution." Kansas was divided, however. And the result was an ugly confrontation, a period of brutal conflict between pro- and anti-slavery forces.

A thirty-three-year-old born in Ohio but who moved to Kansas with his brothers, John Brown, Jr., wrote to his father describing the thugs that had streamed into the territory to promote slavery as "the meanest and most desperate of men, armed to the teeth with Revolvers, Bowie Knives, Rifles & Cannon." He accurately described many of them as being on the payroll of southern slave owners. The father of John Brown, Jr., joined him in Kansas in the fall of 1855. He came bearing a wagonload of weapons and a conviction that he was entering a battle with satanic forces.

The elder Brown was an anti-slavery zealot, to be sure, as were his sons. But Brown's treatment by history, including his portrayal in popular films and fiction, has often overemphasized his extremism rather than thoughtfully examining whether that zeal was warranted given the cause for which he was fighting: bringing an end to an abomination that inflicted the worst kinds of physical and mental torture to the almost 4 million men, women, and children who lived in bondage in America at that time. (The 1860 U.S. Census counted 3,953,762 slaves among the 31,443,321 people in the United States, so they made up 12.6 percent of the population—slightly more than the population of the country's biggest state at the time, New York.) In fact, it could well be argued that it was a time that called for extreme action, and Brown's actions—which would ultimately have him tried and convicted for treason, murder, and insurrection— were also widely hailed at the time. Frederick Douglass, with whom he had a close relationship, would ultimately characterize Brown as a "brave and I believe good man."

In the spring of 1856, however, what was on display was Brown's zeal. May was a particularly fraught month. Pro-slavery gunmen ransacked Lawrence, Kansas. Meanwhile, in Washington, D.C., on May 19 and 20, Massachusetts senator Charles Sumner went to the floor of the U.S. Senate and made a passionate plea for Kansas to be admitted to the Union as a free state. He was particularly brutal in his attack on the Kansas-Nebraska Act and its chief authors, Senators Andrew Butler of South Carolina and Stephen A. Douglas of Illinois. In the speech, he mocked the courtly Butler, characterizing slavery as his mistress who "though ugly to others, is always lovely to him; though polluted in the sight of the world, is chaste in his sight."

Two days later, indicative of the level of tension in the country at the time, Representative Preston Brooks, a cousin of Butler's, confronted Sumner—again on the Senate floor—and said, "Mr.

Sumner, I have read your speech twice over carefully. It is a libel on South Carolina and Mr. Butler, who is a relative of mine." He then took his cane and began beating Sumner on the head. Sumner struggled to fight back but could not, blinded by his own blood. He was bludgeoned into unconsciousness. A friend of Brooks's, another member of Congress named Laurence Keitt, kept those who would help Sumner at bay with a pistol and his own cane.

Sumner survived. The attack won sympathy for the new, abolitionist, party of which he was a member, called the Republicans. And the nation was further inflamed, including Brown, who was outraged at the inability of free states to stop the scourge of slavery. In retaliation, he led a small party of men to a group of cabins that stood on the shores of Pottawatomie Creek in Kansas. There he found five men who were known to be pro-slavery, and he and the others hacked them to death with swords. Kansas was lawless at the time, and Brown escaped capture. One of his sons, Frederick, was not so lucky. He was gunned down in reprisal for the attack.

Brown's commitment to helping win what he saw as the war against slavery only grew more intense. By 1858 he was on the move out of Kansas. His plan was to work to overthrow the institution by force if necessary. His plan was to lead an invasion of a small abolitionist army into the South, where they would then be joined by runaway slaves who would want to fight for their own freedom. He met with abolitionists to win support for his plan. One was Harriet Tubman, the former slave who also had taken matters into her own hands, leading groups of slaves out of the South and on to freedom in the North via the underground railway. The two were kindred spirits, and Tubman, too, hailed Brown. A biographer of hers, Kate Clifford

Larson, asserts that Tubman "thought Brown was the greatest white man who ever lived."

With financial support from rich abolitionists from the Northeast, he purchased rifles and pikes, which he hoped would be the armaments utilized by his invasion army. He met with Douglass to lay out his plan. While Douglass was encouraging, he did not play a hands-on role in Brown's raid on the South.

In 1859, Brown led a much smaller group than he had hoped would coalesce around him, twenty-one men, into the small industrial town of Harpers Ferry, Virginia. His goal was to seize an armory there and then to continue onward, seeking to recruit the slave army that would enable him to overthrow the government of Virginia and begin his undoing of the South and its systems that were so anathema to him. He achieved, briefly, modest success, downing telegraph wires and seizing a few small buildings. But very quickly, federal and local forces converged on Brown, and he and his men were trapped in a small brick firehouse. He lost several men in the action.

The army unit that surrounded him to put down his insurrection was commanded by a colonel whose family was Virginia royalty. He was descended from Revolutionary War heroes, and his wife was the great-granddaughter of Martha Washington, step-great-granddaughter of George Washington. His name was Robert E. Lee. A young first lieutenant under his command was sent under a white flag to negotiate Brown's surrender. When the conflagration sparked in part by this incident led him to leave the U.S. Army, the young officer, J. E. B. Stuart, would return to Lee's side as his most brilliant cavalry commander. Brown rebuffed the attempt at negotiations, and the military took what became known as John Brown's Fort by force, battering down the doors and taking Brown captive. There had been several casualties, including two more of Brown's sons.

Within nine days, Brown's trial in Charles Town, Virginia, began. While he was not charged with federal crimes, prosecutors asserted he was guilty of the crime of treason against the state of Virginia, even though he did not live there (as his defenders unsuccessfully argued). He was found guilty on November 2, 1859, after a jury deliberation that lasted less than an hour. He was sentenced to a public hanging one month later.

His case was a cause célèbre. Great writers of the time, from Ralph Waldo Emerson to Victor Hugo, acclaimed him as a hero, and Hugo argued that he should be pardoned, warning that if he was not it would "certainly shake the whole American democracy."

On the morning of the day of his death, Brown wrote that he was "now quite certain that the crimes of this guilty land will never be purged away but with blood." Onlookers at his execution included another future Confederate general, at the time a senior officer at a local military academy, Thomas "Stonewall" Jackson. Also in the crowd was a well-known actor who also would have a role to play in the conflagration that the hanging of Brown would soon help spark. He was in a costume of sorts, having borrowed a military uniform so he could witness the hanging. His name was John Wilkes Booth. So it is that while some moments that are given great weight by history pass fleetingly, others are freighted with the casts and sets of the great dramas they are. This one was even seen to include celestial portents. In his poem "Year of Meteors," Walt Whitman wrote of "the strange huge meteor procession, dazzling and clear, shooting

over our heads" that marked the year of Brown's death and of
the election of a new president, Abraham Lincoln:

> *Year of meteors! brooding year!*
> *I would bind in words retrospective, some of your*
> > *deeds and signs;*
> *I would sing your contest for the 19th Presidentiad;*
> *I would sing how an old man, tall, with white hair,*
> > *mounted the scaffold in Virginia;*
> *(I was at hand—silent I stood, with teeth shut*
> > *close—I watch'd;*
> *I stood very near you, old man, cool and indiffer-*
> > *ent, but trembling with age and*
> *your unheal'd wounds, you mounted the scaffold)*

Whitman, too, was in the crowd, watching. All knew the
country was a tinderbox. Later, Frederick Douglass, who was
accused by one of Brown's men of conspiring with them but
then failing to live up to his promises of support, would give
a speech asserting that the moment of Brown's "defeat was the
hour of his triumph"; he continued that Brown's "capture" was
the "victory of his life."

He said this two decades after the fact, because while
Brown may have been seen to slavery-supporting Virginians
and perhaps to Southerners everywhere as a traitor, to those in
the North he was not only a hero but a man who by virtue of the
courage of his convictions, of his willingness to act even when
the odds were hugely against him, helped bring about change
that ultimately achieved his dream of the freeing of the slaves
and the end of slavery.

A MOULDERING IN THE GRAVE

From the perspective of our examination of the nature of traitors, treason, and betrayal in American history, with Brown we see someone whose spirit of is more like that of the founders of the country—who were themselves traitors to the British Crown—than it is with others who sought to turn their backs on America in order to advance their own self-interest or to serve foreign masters. He was a hero and very quickly became a martyr.

Troops marched into battle during the earliest days of the Civil War singing an 1861 song that began as follows:

> *John Brown's body lies a mouldering in the grave,*
> *John Brown's body lies a mouldering in the grave,*
> *John Brown's body lies a mouldering in the grave,*
> *His soul's marching on!*

> *Glory Hally, Hallelujah! Glory Hally Hallelujah!*
> *Glory Hally Hallelujah!*
> *His soul's marching on!*

It says something that the song became so synonymous with the cause of the Union that different versions appeared, one of which remains an American anthem to this day, the version of the tune that includes the lyrics of Julia Ward Howe and is known as the "Battle Hymn of the Republic."

But for all the passions triggered by the death of Brown in the North, we also have seen that the strains between North and South had been growing for nearly a century by the time the Civil War started. And within the South—with a lineage that

ran from Jefferson and Madison to Calhoun and his fellow South
Carolinians Butler and Brooks and on to Lee, Stuart, Jackson,
Booth, and the others who gathered to watch Brown hang—
there were also deeply held beliefs in both the sanctity of the
idea of states' rights that underpinned secession as well as in the
much darker and more repulsive cultural flaws and economic
interests that fueled, embraced, and defended slavery.

Like Robert E. Lee and Stonewall Jackson, later commem-
orated with Jefferson Davis on the side of a mountain at Stone
Mountain, Georgia, Davis began his public career as a student at
the U.S. Military Academy and subsequently served in the U.S.
Army with distinction. All three would fight in the Mexican-
American War. But unlike Lee and Jackson, Davis was drawn
to politics early.

Davis was elected to Congress at the age of thirty-seven,
even before his service in the war with Mexico, during which
he distinguished himself at the battles of Monterrey and Buena
Vista. He had to step down from the House of Representatives
to serve, but two years later, in 1847, he was appointed to the
Senate representing Mississippi. Within six years he was serving in the Franklin Pierce administration as secretary of war, a
post where he earned Washington-wide respect as an effective
cabinet officer. He served a second Senate term thereafter, but
that was truncated when, on January 21, 1861, he was compelled
to resign as Mississippi joined the other states of the South in seceding from the Union. A month later, the newly convened Confederate Congress selected him as president of the Confederacy.

Robert E. Lee would remain a Union Army officer for several more months. His mentor, General Winfield Scott, was
commanding general of the army, and he promised Lee an im-

portant command, promoting him to colonel and making him commander of the First Cavalry. However, Lee viewed himself first and foremost as a Virginian, and when Virginia voted to secede on April 17, his divided loyalties presented him with a deep quandary. Lee's superiors in the army felt that they had to sweeten their offer to keep the talented Lee from taking a position with the Confederate Army. He was offered the rank of major general and commander of the forces defending Washington, D.C.

Lee declined, saying, "I look upon secession as anarchy. If I owned the four millions of slaves in the South I would sacrifice them all to the Union; but how can I draw my sword upon Virginia, my native state?"

Efforts to persuade him to remain a Union officer were in vain. Though Lee's family later reported that he struggled for several days with the decision whether to leave the army that had been his only professional home. He submitted his letter of resignation on April 20, devastating Scott. Within days, Virginia had put him in command of the state's forces, giving him as a symbol of his authority a sword once owned by his wife's step-great-grandfather, George Washington. Many of his relatives, including his sons, chose to join him in fighting for the South, but some did not; Virginia was riven from border to border by such hard decisions concerning whether to place loyalty to state or nation first.

When the Confederate Army was established Lee became one of its first five generals, although he did not rise to command of the entire army until very near the end of the war. Unlike Davis, who started out quite popular but lost his appeal to the public, thanks to his rather dry personality and a tendency to reward those closest to him, Lee started off slowly, and it was not until successes at the helm of what he had dubbed the Army of Northern Virginia—pushing Yankee troops back from Richmond and winning victories in the Seven Days Battles and then at the Second Battle of Bull Run—that he began to be seen with the respect and even reverence of his men and the public as well.

Thomas Jackson, whose VMI students had manned two artillery pieces at John Brown's hanging, achieved even earlier acclaim for his battlefield exploits than had Lee. Promoted to colonel and on April 27, 1861, put in command at the site of Brown's raid, Harpers Ferry, Jackson put together a brigade that he drilled with the seriousness the devout Presbyterian brought to every pursuit. The success of his men in early raids led to his promotion to brigadier general by June. A month later, in the First Battle of Bull Run, his troops' resoluteness earned him the nickname "Stonewall" and, less than three months later, a promotion to major general.

Lee considered Jackson his "right hand" and said as much after Jackson was wounded by friendly fire after the Battle of Chancellorsville, resulting initially in the loss of one of Jackson's arms. Within days he was dead.

The loss may have been a turning point in the Confederacy's fortunes. Some historians speculate that his absence contributed to the defeat suffered by Lee's forces six weeks later at Gettysburg, which, as it turned out was the beginning of the end for the Confederacy. By the winter of 1865, matters were dire as Lee was named by Davis to be general in chief of the Armies of the Confederate States. Losses had been heavy and thoughts had turned to the unthinkable—arming the slaves and granting those who might serve with a path to freedom.

Before putting this plan into effect, Lee was forced by Union pressure to abandon his Richmond headquarters, and on April 9, following the Battle of Appomattox Court House, he surrendered to the Union commander, Ulysses S. Grant. In his farewell address, Lee pleaded for his troops to give up the fight and for a national healing to begin. He also welcomed the end of slavery.

This conciliatory spirit rather remarkably echoed the victors' from the North. There was a deep desire to heal the wounds of war and to knit the nation back together, especially now that the principle of the primacy of the federal government and every individual's overarching obligation of loyalty to the Union was established. Lincoln, before his assassination, feared that anything less than such an effort would result in suppurating wounds that might not heal and might make the grievous losses of the war for naught.

Lee and the other commanders of the Confederacy were not punished as traitors, though no doubt traitors they were. Some lost the right to vote, and some, like Lee, their property (his mansion overlooking the city of Washington was claimed by the government, and its grounds were used for a new national cemetery; the house, built by his wife's father, George Washington's stepson, was called Arlington House, and the new cemetery still bears the name Arlington). Lee applied to have his citizenship restored, and while his request was at first rejected, by Christmas Day of 1868, Lincoln's successor, President Andrew Johnson, had declared a sweeping amnesty that resulted in the restoration of Lee's citizenship and a pardon. Johnson's proclamation effectively resulted in the pardon of all Lee's fellow rebels from the crime of treason—despite the fact that their acts were certainly the most clear instance of "levying War against [the United States], or in adhering to [our] Enemies, giving them Aid and Comfort." By that time, Lee was president of Washington College in Lexington, Virginia (later known as Washington and Lee University).

While Davis was captured after the end of the war and imprisoned, by May 1867 he was offered release on $100,000 bail. The money was put up by a cross section of the country's richest men, who felt that, again, the release of Davis would facilitate further healing and who noted also that he had been denied a speedy trial. In part, the reason he was denied the trial was that many senior federal officials were worried that Davis would have made the case that his secession was constitutionally permitted, pointing to the arguments of Jefferson or Madison in Federalist No. 46 about the relative power of state governments. Worse, they feared that Davis might actually prevail, and they did not wish to establish that precedent in the courts.

Among those who underwrote Davis's bond was Gerrit Smith, one of the secret financiers of Brown's raid on Harpers Ferry. Another was New York publisher Horace Greeley, who when confronted by the anger of fellow New Yorkers at what he and the others had done, argued passionately that such gestures were essential. "Gentlemen," he is quoted as saying, "I arraign you as narrow-minded blockheads, who would like to be useful to a great and good cause, but don't know how. Your attempt to base a great, enduring party on the hate and wrath necessarily engendered by a bloody civil war, is as though you should plant a colony on an iceberg which had somehow drifted into a tropical ocean."

Davis, like Lee, would go on to a peaceful life, enjoying for almost a quarter century after the end of the Civil War the acclaim of fellow southerners and a remarkable degree of respectability. He ran an insurance company, wrote a defense of his actions, was offered a university presidency, and was a frequent speech giver and honoree at events across the South.

Lee, too, was hailed, even more so. From commemoration on U.S. postage stamps (once with Davis and twice with Stonewall Jackson), to acclaim as a brilliant military mind, his post–Civil War reputation was, until relatively recently, glittering. As noted earlier with Davis and Jackson, among the many monuments to him is the gigantic stone relief carving of the three astride their horses on the side of Stone Mountain in Georgia, a site that is to this day the most visited tourist attraction in the state.

AN ENDURING HISTORY OF WHITE NATIONALISM

No doubt much of the celebration of these men took place in the revival of white nationalist views that came in the wake of Reconstruction and really began to flourish in the first decades of the twentieth century. Celebrating the Confederacy and its heroes was a way of promoting a vile racist ideology. It is a sign of how virulent that racism is, how deeply ingrained in America's history and character it is, that to this day the phenomenon continues. Indeed, fighting to preserve Confederate monuments, even as they started to be pulled down in just the past few years, became a way for President Trump and other leading Republicans (the party that, despite its anti-slavery origins, has come in recent decades to most embrace many of the views it was established to combat) to signal to their own white nationalist supporters that they were with them. (As I mentioned earlier, much of this book was written at my home in Alexandria, Virginia, not two blocks away from the house in which Lee grew up. While I was writing it, the town decided to remove Jefferson Davis's name from a highway running through the community—but a statue honoring the soldiers of the Confederacy remains up in the middle of the community, and every home once owned or occupied by the Lee family features plaques celebrating them.)

But we, studying how the United States and history view traitors and acts of betrayal, need to also note that part of the sentiment that led to pardoning the leaders of the Confederacy was tied to the deep roots in our history of the philosophical reasons they believed they had the right to separate themselves from the United States, and was as much established by the words and deeds of our founders as were the other oldest institutions of the U.S. government. Further, there was a sense that while these men were traitors to the United States, they were acting out of a different sort of—profoundly wrong, deeply misguided—loyalty, but one that was nonetheless understandable in a way that cleaving to a foreign power would not be, could not be.

Indeed, after the death of Brown, who was hung for the treasonous act of advocating what was right and what would be the official motive behind the U.S. federal government's position in the war to follow, the only other person who was convicted and punished for treason during the prosecution of the Civil War was an impulsive New Orleans Confederate sympathizer by the name of William Mumford, who, in 1862, made the mistake of trying to tear down the Union flag from a flagpole in New Orleans against the orders of the Union commander seizing the town. He was summarily tried for treason and hanged to set an example for others in the city.

Of course, at the war's end, just days after Lee's surrender at Appomattox, that young actor who had been lurking, dressed as a militiaman, in the shadows of John Brown's scaffold, would play his great part in our history by assassinating Abraham

Lincoln. While John Wilkes Booth would later die while trying to escape the Union troops that pursued him in the wake of his attack at Ford's Theater, his coconspirators in the Lincoln murder plot were not so lucky. Their plot, which was initially conceived the year before, involved a plan to kidnap Lincoln and bring him to Richmond, but was altered in the last days of the war into an effort to decapitate the entire government. It included plans to murder the vice president, Andrew Johnson, and Secretary of State William Seward (because, it was later alleged, there was a belief the Constitution had no provision for who would rule should all three die, and so at that point the country would be left without a leader), but it was so badly bungled that within days eight alleged conspirators were captured.

The days leading up to the assassination were an emotional time for the country. Flower garlands and parties and church services celebrated the end of the war. Newspapers across the country ran editorials pleading for healing. *The New York Times* wrote, "The hour of victory is the hour for clemency, always the hour for the easiest winning of the hearts of the vanquished."

Some in the North did not immediately embrace this spirit, notable among them Johnson, who, days before Lincoln's death, called for Davis to be hanged, a call that was met with enthusiastic shouts of "Hang him!" from the crowd. (Hotheaded crowds stirred up by demagogic leaders are, as we in our own era know, an enduring feature of American life.).

Meanwhile, for many supporters of the South, the defeat was bitter. For Booth and his coconspirators the surrender of Lee's armies created a sense of urgency. They felt they had to act or all would be lost. Then, when Lincoln was murdered and Seward wounded, the fierce desire for revenge entered the picture. A military guard assigned to Andrew Johnson described him as pacing back and forth declaring, "They shall suffer for this! They shall suffer for this!" Grant later would write, "He seemed to be anxious to get at the leaders to punish them. He would say that the leaders of the rebellion must be punished, and that treason must be made odious." Elsewhere, men who declared that Lincoln got what he deserved were summarily gunned down by angry citizens, in more than one instance.

Indeed, it was immediately concluded that the attack on Lincoln had to be part of a plot that was approved by Jefferson Davis. High-ranking officials in the government agreed with Johnson that the crime itself would provide an opportunity to bring real justice. That is why, in a controversial decision still debated to this day, it was decided by Secretary of War Edwin Stanton that the conspirators would be tried by a military tribunal. His reasoning was that despite the surrender, hostilities had not altogether ended and that therefore the actions of Booth and the others were under military rather than civil jurisdiction. The fact that it was believed that the murder was an official plot brought about by Davis's government under the supervision of its secret services only further warranted this decision in their minds. Elsewhere it was seen as a mistake, an invitation to make martyrs of the murderers, and, in the view of some, such as the editors of the *New-York Tribune,* as unconstitutional. A former attorney general, Edward Bates, wrote, "If the offenders are done to death by the tribunal, however truly guilty, they will pass for martyrs with half the world." In the South, it was viewed as a sign that the trial would be a sham. A nine-man tribunal was named to oversee the trial, and the unmistakable message they received from their superiors was that justice was to be swift.

The conspirators were held in prison, shackled and hooded at all times, including later when they were brought to court.

There, 271 witnesses were brought before the court. They described—some with testimony later thought to be of dubious authenticity—how the plan was hatched as part of a series of terrorist efforts by the Confederate Secret Service to destabilize the North. These included attacks on buildings, the kidnapping plot, and even an alleged bioterror attack centering on the distribution of clothing exposed to deadly diseases. Booth and the others were alleged to be funded by the Confederate government and their plan approved at the highest levels.

Despite the dubious nature of some of the testimony and the circumstantial nature of some of the evidence against some of the accused, the court did show a degree of leniency, recommending that four of those involved, but not closest to the center of the plot, be imprisoned. The core conspirators were convicted of "maliciously, unlawfully, and traitorously" conspiring to kill Lincoln. Again, given the challenges of making a formal "treason" accusation, and the strength of the case on the underlying crimes, the specific charges stopped short of using that term— though it was regularly used throughout the trial to describe the behavior of the men (and even in one instance of the lawyer for one of the accused). Of the four who were ultimately hanged, one of those, Mary Surratt, owner of the boardinghouse where much of the plot was alleged to have been hatched and where two of the conspirators stayed, was seen as a special case because she was a woman and the evidence against her was not as clear-cut. Five members of the tribunal recommended that her death sentence be commuted. It is unclear whether this recommendation was ever seen by President Johnson, but in the end, he took no action in the forty-eight hours between her conviction and her hanging. She thus became the first woman ever executed by the U.S. government.

The critics of choosing the course of tribunal should have been listened to. (Not an irrelevant point in a country that only recently sought to suspend normal criminal due process in the face of terrorists, as we shall see as we consider more recent cases of treason in the next chapter.)

Former congressman Henry Winter Davis wrote, "I cannot refrain from expressing to you my conviction that the trial of the persons charged with the conspiracy against President Lincoln and Secretary Seward by Military Commission will prove disastrous to yourself your administration and your supporters who may attempt to apologize for it." As Thomas Turner wrote in 1982 for the *Journal of the Abraham Lincoln Association*, "These words sound prophetic for it was not long before Johnson's enemies, who were trying to impeach him, were charging that Johnson might have been involved in Lincoln's death and that he use the military trial to enforce silence."

In this controversy and the cases that immediately preceded it during the Civil War era, several core themes that arise in our consideration of past traitorous acts in light of those of the current administration are underscored. First, the formal charge of treason is seldom made. Next, our government(s)—federal and state—often trim their reading of the law to suit the prevailing political winds of the time. Additionally, the cases made in courts are often incomplete or colored by the mood of the moment or the objectives of political leaders. Finally, while the verdicts of courts are final, as they were for those convicted of treasonous acts (if not treason itself), from Brown to Mumford to Booth and his coconspirators, those verdicts are often overturned in the court of public opinion as perspective is gained. Traitors who escape the harsh verdicts of courts, like Burr or Wilkinson or Davis or Lee, are as likely to later be deemed guilty of high crimes against the United States—much as those who are convicted, like Brown (or even, in light of some historical debate about the evidence presented against her, like Mary Surratt), are granted pardons by history and even, in the case of Brown, ultimately seen as heroes.

4

THE SHADOW OF DOUBT

Traitors are hated even by those whom they prefer.

—Tacitus

Betrayal is not an American invention. Ancient history has given us the examples of Ephialtes of Trachis, who sold out the Greeks to the Persians at the Battle of Thermopylae; Judas Iscariot; and Caesar's one-time friend Brutus. But diverse, open societies that both encourage dissent and draw their citizens from every corner of the globe invite more instances of conflicting views and the perception of divided loyalties or worse.

The earliest days of the United States saw this with the cases of some who had lasting loyalties to the British, like Benedict Arnold, or those who were drawn to the French, like Edmund Randolph, or those who would sell their loyalties to the highest bidder, as was the case with James Wilkinson and the Spanish. During the nineteenth century, America became seen as a beacon of opportunity to those who faced oppression, famine, and economic struggles around the world. Starting in the wake of the Great European Famine in the 1840s, the United States attracted large communities of immigrants from Britain, Ireland, Germany, Scandinavia, Italy, and Greece. Later came Jews from eastern Europe, then Chinese, Japanese, Lebanese, and Syrians added to the mix.

By the late nineteenth century, almost 14 percent of the U.S. population was foreign-born, a number slightly higher than it is today. Among these was Frederick Trump, a young man trained as a barber, who fled his native Bavaria to avoid military service. (It runs in the family.)

Trump came to the United States to make his fortune and ultimately did in the booming Pacific Northwest and the Yukon by offering room, board, and prostitutes to miners and others trying to make their fortune. Although he tried to return home to Bavaria in the wake of his first successes, the Bavarian government expelled him from the country by royal decree as a draft dodger, and he landed again on American shores, settling in New York City. He was one of the successful ones. But like many immigrants, he was never looked at as fully American by many of his neighbors (who had seemingly forgotten their own origins). It made his life uncomfortable as the United States entered World War I and German immigrants and those from the Austro-Hungarian Empire were viewed as untrustworthy. Later, the pressure would be so uncomfortable for his son, Fred, during World War II, that he would say that the family was not from Kallstadt in the Kingdom of Bavaria, but rather from Karlstad in Sweden (a lie that was later repeated as fact by his veracity challenged son Donald in his book *The Art of the Deal*.)

As tempting as it is to succumb to sympathy for the poor immigrant Trump family and their having to deal with nationalist prejudice in the United States, they were not alone. As the United States became a global actor, issues of dual allegiance increasingly plagued the paranoid and created opportunities for demagogues. This began with the war that established the United States as one of the planet's great powers, World War I.

Today, in yet another illustration of the shifting views of history toward past leaders and their actions, we have begun to reassess the president who once was acclaimed for leading America during the time of what was then known as the Great War and would surpass the U.S. Civil War to become by far the most brutal conflagration mankind had ever seen. Woodrow Wilson—who for years was seen not only as a great wartime leader but also as an intellectual pillar among presidents (he was the president of the university that Aaron Burr's father had helped to found, Princeton) and a pioneer of multilateralism, given his advocacy for the League of Nations—has more recently received well-warranted criticism for his lifelong record of racism.

Wilson, the first southerner elected to the presidency since Zachary Taylor, thirteen years before the start of the Civil War, himself a proud descendant of warriors for the South's "Lost Cause," oversaw the resegregation of the federal government, wholesale firings of black federal employees, and was a champion of a group that would later be joined by Donald Trump's father Fred Trump, the Ku Klux Klan. Wilson had written in his *A History of the American People,* "The white men of the South were aroused by the mere instinct of self-preservation to rid themselves, by fair means or foul, of the intolerable burden of governments sustained by the votes of ignorant negroes and conducted in the interest of adventurers . . . until at last there had sprung into existence a great *Ku Klux Klan,* an 'Invisible Empire of the South,' . . . to protect the southern country."

But his prejudices extended far beyond his contempt for African Americans. Once Congress granted his request for a declaration of war on April 2, 1917, he encouraged sweeping efforts to target, monitor, arrest, and detain those he felt might be disloyal—German Americans, former residents of the Austro-Hungarian Empire, even Irish Americans who might not be willing to support America's ally, Great Britain. He also felt that radicals whose views were antiwar should be targeted. He had revealed these views even before the start of the war, when he said, "There are citizens of the United States, I blush to admit, born under other flags . . . who have poured the poison of disloyalty into the very arteries of our national life. . . . Such creatures of passion, disloyalty, and anarchy must be crushed out."

Within those words we see the classic and pernicious conflation of perceived threats that enables demagogues to overstate them, stir fear, and at the same time target not just those who may pose a real threat but others who have an agenda that might for other reasons be anathema to the powers doing the targeting. The arithmetic was simple. Germany was the enemy. Therefore German Americans were a threat. But so, too, were those who might weaken us by other means, like union members or those who opposed war or sought to weaken the establishment, like anarchists or leftists. It is aped today as we target not just potential terrorists who might infiltrate our borders, but if many of those terrorists are Muslims, then all Muslims; and then if Muslims are brown and foreign, then all brown, foreign people.

Germans who, like Frederick Trump, were born overseas were rounded up and interned. But union members were also especially targeted. (The growth of the union movement was seen as deeply alarming to the Washington establishment and its plutocratic benefactors.)

Anti-German sentiment swept the country. As the Trumps would later do, many Germans denied their heritage or even changed their names. In a wonderful summary of this era in *The New York Review of Books* describing this moment, Adam Hochschild writes:

> *Families named Schmidt quickly became Smith. German-language textbooks were tossed on bonfires. The German-born conductor of the Boston Symphony Orchestra, Karl Muck, was locked up, even though he was a citizen of Switzerland; notes he had made on a score of the* St. Matthew passion *were suspected of being coded messages to Germany. Berlin, Iowa, changed its name to Lincoln, and East Germantown, Indiana, became Pershing, after the general leading American soldiers in the broad-brimmed hats to France. Hamburger was now "Salisbury steak" and German measles "Liberty measles." The* New York Herald *published the names and addresses of every German or Austro-Hungarian national living in the city.*

Lynchings followed. A far-too-sweeping crackdown on the media targeted publications including content that might "embarrass" the country. And union members suffered especially. Their publications were shut down. Members were arrested, made examples of, tarred and feathered. If this sounds exactly like the treatment of bitter divisions and tactics of revolutionary or Civil War America, it is because it was. When we see this treatment today, we often hear people say, "This is not America." But it is. This is a side to America that recurs throughout our history. What's more, it is not just the America of mobs. It is the America of elites—as it was when Adams passed the Alien and Sedition Acts during the Quasi-War (to reduce immigration, to make criticism of the government a lie), or when Mumford was hanged by a senior Union general for treason for taking down an American flag in 1862. One of the blue bloods of America's elite, Elihu Root, a Nobel Prize winner who had served as secretary of state and was chairman of the Carnegie Endowment for International Peace (under whose auspices I began the process of writing this book), is cited in the Hochschild article as saying to a New York audience, "There are men walking about the streets of this city tonight who ought to be taken out at sunrise tomorrow and shot. There are some newspapers published in this city every day the editors of which deserve conviction and execution for treason."

While the real examples of espionage during the war were few and far between, and there were no cases of the U.S. government charging anyone with treason during that time, the views of Wilson, Root, and their associates enabled the government to target other groups and to sow the seeds of distrust across America, by which the taint of treason or betrayal could be applied to others who were merely trying to eke out a living or improve their ways of life. When the war ended, the attitude of distrust and targeting shifted to those who might be seen to carry the risk of bringing to America what was happening in Russia: Communist revolution. This threat was seen by the American establishment as even more dangerous than that of Germany. Black soldiers returning from war and expecting the gratitude of their nation were seen by Wilson and others as potential advocates for "Bolshevism" in America. The result was a spike in lynchings and more energy to fuel the resurgent racism of the Klan and groups like it across America.

Leftists and union leaders were often one and the same, and they were charged by the government in wave after wave of raids that resulted in the arrests of thousands. And while the government was so effective that union membership plummeted and the American Socialist Party was hobbled, the mindset that confronting a union was fundamentally a patriotic act persisted long after the end of World War II.

In fact, the one American who was tried and convicted of treason at the time had been rounded up for taking part in a protest by miners at Blair Mountain, West Virginia, in 1921. This protest, turned into a confrontation that ultimately would become the biggest labor uprising in American history. Sparked by armed confrontations between union miners and opponents who sought to maintain nonunion mines in the region, the conflict escalated to the point that it became the largest armed uprising in the United States since the Civil War. Almost ten thousand armed coal miners were confronted by thousands of strikebreakers, and, ultimately, when President Warren Harding saw events spiraling out of control, by the U.S. Army. As many as one hundred died.

Among the almost one thousand miners who were subsequently arrested, the charges ranged from murder to conspiracy to committing murder to treason against the state of West Virginia. One of those charged with the latter crime, a forty-one-year-old leader of the miners named Walter Allen, was charged with treason against the state of West Virginia. His trial took place in the same courthouse in Charles Town, West Virginia, where John Brown had been tried and condemned to die. Testimony against him described that he exhorted miners to action in mass meetings, that he had overseen votes to take action, acquired weapons and financing for the miners' efforts, and that he was active throughout the conflict. The leader of the United Mine Workers, Bill Blizzard, was charged with similar crimes. But at Blizzard's trial his lawyers effectively argued that the miners' actions were warranted by the brutality of the anti-union forces and he was acquitted. Not so fortunate, Allen was found guilty on September 16, 1922.

As it happened, Allen was released on a $10,000 bond pending appeal. He was never heard from again.

FROM AXIS SALLY TO TOKYO ROSE

The second global conflict the United States was to face in the twentieth century was to raise many of the same concerns and trigger many of the same, often reprehensible, tactics concerning loyalty to the United States as did the First World War. The internment camps in which Japanese American citizens were kept during the war is one of the darkest chapters in modern American history. But in addition to such hideous race-based, fearmonger-driven excesses and abuses, World War II saw a number of cases of Americans charged with treason for working alongside our foreign enemies in Germany, Italy, and Japan.

Because, of course, even though the vast majority of the German Americans whose loyalty to the United States was questioned during the First World War and then after were upstanding citizens, some were not. Max and Erna Haupt came to the United States in the wake of the hard feelings associated with World War I. Max, a veteran of the Kaiser's Army, came in 1923. His wife and his son, Herbert, arrived two years later. The family became U.S. citizens seven years after that.

Once young Herbert reached the age of twenty-one, he wanted to set off and see the world. At least, that was his story. He and a friend exited the United States via the Mexican border and headed straight for the German embassy in Mexico City, where they applied for and received German passports. From there they made their way to Germany and into the service of

Adolf Hitler's government. After distinguishing himself as a civilian coast watcher, Herbert was recruited to join a group of a dozen others to return to the United States and spy on behalf of the Germany government. He and the others made the return trip to the United States via U-boat.

While Haupt returned home to Chicago to see his family, two other members of the group had a change of heart and turned themselves in to the FBI. They identified their associates, and all were rounded up and arrested, including Haupt's parents.

Once again, because the United States was at war, it was determined that Haupt and seven other members of his spy ring should face a military tribunal. (The precedent of this case was later cited by the Bush administration when they asserted such tribunals could and should be used in the case of terrorists in the early twenty-first century.) Six of the defendants were found guilty of being enemy agents and sentenced to die in the electric chair. Haupt was among them.

Meanwhile, the government decided to send a message to others who might be sympathizing with America's overseas enemies, and it charged Haupt's parents with treason for not turning their son in. While Erna was released and deported following her conviction, Hans received a life sentence. He was later released and deported in 1957.

Harsh though these punishments were, they did not deter a small number of Americans from seeking to support the war efforts of America's enemies. Among these was Martin James Monti, a U.S. Army Air Forces pilot who defected in his aircraft to the Waffen-SS in 1944. He was convicted of treason and paroled in 1960. Another was Tomoya Kawakita, an American of Japanese descent, who was attending university in Japan when the war broke out. He was put into service as an interpreter at a forced-labor camp that employed prisoners of war in mining and metal-processing jobs. After the war he returned to the United States but was recognized and charged with multiple counts of treason. His jury was instructed that if he was aware of his U.S. citizenship and his duty to the United States, then he should be found guilty of treason. After long deliberations, he was found guilty on eight of the thirteen counts of treason with which he had been charged. He appealed the case, and it went all the way to the U.S. Supreme Court, where the verdict against him was upheld despite the dissent of three justices who argued that during the war, while Kawakita had shown support for Japan, "as a matter of law, he expatriated himself as well as can be done," thus accepting the arguments of Kawakita's lawyers that he was effectively no longer a U.S. citizen at the time and therefore could not be convicted of treason. President Eisenhower commuted Kawakita's death sentence to life imprisonment and then, shortly before his assassination, John F. Kennedy allowed him to leave the United States and return to Japan, where he lived for many decades afterward in obscurity.

But the greatest and most notable of the treason cases in the United States during the Second World War came in the instances of Americans with foreign sympathies who ultimately served the propaganda efforts of the Axis Powers. They betrayed their country much as Trump later would, by disseminating disinformation on behalf of foreign adversaries of the United States. Among these was Iva Toguri D'Aquino, who like Kawakita was an American of Japanese descent who found herself visiting relatives in Japan when war broke out and who ultimately became one of several female propaganda broadcasters for the Japanese who were dubbed "Tokyo Rose" by American troops, playing American music and offering subversive stories designed to undermine the morale of soldiers and sailors stationed in the Pacific. In a similar role, Mildred Gillars, an itinerant American would-be actress and artist's model, who made her way to Germany from where she grew up in Ohio and, once the war started, began to broadcast as "Axis Sally" on behalf of the Germans. Robert Henry Best was a U.S.-born foreign correspondent who broadcast for the Nazis under the name "Mr. Guess Who," and Herbert John Burgman, who did the same broadcasting for the German Radio D.E.B.U.N.K. under the name "Joe Scanlon," were both convicted of treason for spreading Nazi propaganda. The list of those who faced similar charges for broadcasting Nazi propaganda—underscoring the importance of information warfare even during World War II—is much longer and included Frederick W. Kaltenbach, Douglas Chandler, Edward Leo Delaney, Constance Drexel, Jane Anderson, and Max Otto Koischwitz. The poet Ezra Pound similarly was charged with treason for broadcasts made on behalf of the Mussolini regime in Italy.

Gillars, who had been born Mildred Sisk, was captured after the war and indicted in September 1948 on ten counts of treason. She was convicted on just one but was sentenced to ten to thirty years in prison. There is some dispute over whether she or Mary Surratt was the first woman to be convicted of treason against the United States. She was released after becoming eligible for parole in 1961. Burgman was charged with sixty-nine counts of treason. After a trial in which his attorneys argued he was not mentally fit to stand trial, he was convicted on thirteen counts and sentenced to six to twenty years. He died in prison.

Best, who was charged with Kaltenbach, Chandler, Delaney, Drexel, Anderson, Koischwitz, and Pound, was convicted on twelve counts of treason and given a life sentence. It did not last very long. He died in prison in 1952. Kaltenbach was even less fortunate, dying in a Soviet prison camp before he could be tried. Koischwitz suffered a similar fate even earlier, dying in 1944 in a German hospital. Chandler was sentenced to life and got out in 1963. Charges against Delaney and Anderson were dropped for lack of evidence. Drexel, an heiress to a great American fortune, also saw charges dropped when it was concluded her broadcasts for the Nazis were, as she had asserted, primarily on cultural topics. Pound, as a famous poet, became a cause célèbre. He was a noted anti-Semite, and his views were made clear when on the day Germany surrendered he was quoted as comparing Hitler to Joan of Arc, characterizing him as a saint, and saying that Mussolini was "an imperfect character who lost his head." When he was returned to the United States in 1945 he was committed to a psychiatric hospital, where he remained, was visited by famous literary friends, wrote some of his best-known poetry, and where, in fact, he resided until his release in 1958. From there he returned to Italy until his death in 1972. The outrage among some Americans at his behavior was best captured in the words of playwright Arthur Miller, who said, "In his wildest moments of human vilification Hitler never approached our Ezra. . . . He knew all America's weaknesses and played them as expertly as Goebbels ever did."

Pound's case, because of his prominence as a poet and editor, had a major impact on academia. But Miller's critique of him could be directed at all the others, who took their understandings of America and used them against the country at a time of existential war.

One exception was certainly Iva Toguri D'Aquino. While there is little doubt that she did broadcast on behalf of the Japanese, the evidence against her was extremely weak. Investigations would later prove that her two most damaging accusers perjured themselves and were coached in their testimonies. As details of her time in Japan emerged, it became clear that she risked her life seeking to aid American and Allied prisoners of war and that she actually resisted spreading propaganda, offering primarily music and brief comedy sketches. Although she served six years and two months on the one count of treason on which she was found guilty, following an exposé on the U.S. television news program *60 Minutes* she was pardoned by President Gerald Ford. Her citizenship was restored, and in, 2006, the very last year of her life, U.S. veterans actually gave her an award citing "her indomitable spirit, love of country, and the example of courage she has given her fellow Americans." She was yet another example of the overzealous prosecution of the foreign-born or different during times of war or national strife.

RED SCARE

During the years Toguri spent in prison, another such wave of distrust spread through America, associated with a new and different kind of war, the Cold War, which had broken out between the United States and our former allies the Soviets. Much as during World War I, loyalty movements broke out across the country and vigilantism followed; so, too, did the far-right wing in America again seek to attack anyone who was seen as potentially associated with the Russians.

The unease of the American establishment with Communism dates back to the nineteenth century. According to Samuel Bernstein in *The Massachusetts Review*:

> *No political or economic issue in the United States, save governmental Corruption, received more headlines in the American press of the 1870s than did the Paris Commune (the*

*radical socialist government that took over in Paris following
the capture of Napoleon III in 1870) and the International
Workingmen's Association. Every big newspaper gave read-
ers the impression that the foundations of organized society
had crumbled. Anarchy, assassination, slaughter, incendia-
rism, streets covered with human gore—such blood curdling
scenes were monotonously reported in the news.*

As we have seen, with the Russian Revolution in 1917, these
concerns were rekindled, and Socialists, Communists, and their
allies in unions were actively targeted by the government, law-
enforcement, establishment critics, and vigilantes. Concerns
were, on one level, well-founded; within years of the establishment of the Communist government in Moscow, it began an
effort to infiltrate American political life and, working in conjunction with the Communist Party of the United States, began
to siphon out secrets from America while at the same time seeking to destabilize and if possible trigger this country's transition
to Communism. The Russians did this via agents operated by
multiple units of its government, including at different points the
GRU (military intelligence), OGPU (secret police), NKVD (interior ministry), and later the KGB (Committee for State Security).

When the United States entered the Second World War,
the Soviets became a vital ally but never one that was trusted.
Substantial efforts continued throughout the war to monitor
Russian spying, including actively seeking to intercept and de-
code encrypted Soviet messages via a major counterintelligence
operation of the U.S. Army's Signal Intelligence Service, known
as the Venona Project. The project began in 1943 at the height
of World War II and continued until 1980. Via the work of that
project and more recently the opening of Soviet archives since

the collapse of the USSR, we have learned of the staggering scale and scope of Russian espionage and psychological and information warfare efforts in the United States, efforts that we know continue to this day.

War-weary though the United States was as World War II drew to a close, it was clear that the emerging rivalry with the Soviets posed the greatest extant risk of yet another global conflagration and one that, with the advent of atomic weapons, could surpass the toll of even the two ghastly conflicts that had dominated the first half of the twentieth century. America alone had the bomb in 1945 as the war concluded, but the Germans had been rushing to acquire nuclear capability during the war, and it was clear that so, too, were the Soviets. Therefore, as soon as World War II ended, the national security apparatus of the United States reoriented itself to focus on the Russian threat.

Politicians also sought to get in front of the issue. Among the vehicles they used to identify, denounce, and investigate disloyalty to the United States was the House Un-American Activities Committee (HUAC). Established before the war, it played a role in leading the movement to place Japanese Americans in internment camps while also investigating potential Communist infiltration of everything from youth groups to theater companies. Shortly after the war, in 1947, the nine-member committee began to investigate alleged Communist influence in Hollywood. Accused writers, producers, and directors who appeared before the committee and refused to testify were found guilty of contempt of Congress and blacklisted in Hollywood. Ultimately, more than three hundred artists suffered a similar fate, most seeing their careers come permanently to an end.

Then, in the summer of 1948, the committee conducted hearings featuring testimony from confessed former Soviet agents including Elizabeth Bentley, a former librarian who had formed a romantic and professional partnership with the head of a Russian spy ring, later taking it over when he died. Testimony also came from a journalist at *Time* magazine named Whittaker Chambers. The goal was to get the witnesses to name Communist agents. Chambers fingered six in the U.S. government, including two brothers, Alger and Donald Hiss. Hiss denied the allegations, but doubts about his testimony led the committee and notably one recently elected member of Congress and former U.S. Navy veteran eager to make a name for himself—Richard Nixon of California—to dig deeper. The conflicting stories between Hiss and Chambers were ultimately resolved when Chambers and the FBI produced evidence from documents allegedly passed by Hiss to the Russians to film stored in a pumpkin patch and a typewriter that seemed to link Hiss to the documents in question. The result was a conviction of Hiss on two counts of espionage. (One reason that he was not charged with treason was that throughout the time of his alleged spying, the Soviets were actually American allies—there was no enemy there to aid and abet.) He ended up serving three and a half years in prison. He also fought the charges for most of his life, seeking to clear his name. He was partially successful as it became clear that much of the evidence against him was dubious and that, indeed, some had been manufactured (including, according to later reports, the fabrication of the typewriter that was a key element of the prosecution's case—reports that indicated Nixon was among those who helped engineer the results). That said, it is now thought, based on the bulk of the evidence that subsequently became available both through the release of Venona Project documents and other evidence from Soviet archives, that Hiss was in all likelihood guilty of spying for the Russians.

Questions remain. Because regardless of the allegations against Hiss, it was undoubtedly true that prosecutors took liberties with the law and, to put it as gently as possible, wanted to take no chances that Hiss would not be convicted.

Similar liberties—which is to say similar abuses—marked the next major trial associated with Russian espionage in the United States, a case so polarizing that it is perhaps, alongside that of Benedict Arnold, the one that most Americans think of when they think of betraying the United States. It is the case that was ultimately brought against an unassuming Jewish electrical engineer from the Lower East Side of Manhattan and his wife, a former aspiring actress, who met as members of the Young Communist League and were married in 1939. He was Julius Rosenberg. Her name was Ethel Greenglass.

In 1940, Julius Rosenberg went to work for the U.S. Army Signal Corps at Fort Monmouth, New Jersey. There he was exposed to some of the army's most advanced electronic technologies. Two years later, he was recruited by the NKVD to spy. Not only was his mission to provide information associated with his work, but he was also to recruit a network of others to do the same. Rosenberg was apparently quite successful at this and ultimately gathered together a group that harvested information on next-generation aircraft and industrial and manufacturing equipment. When the Russians learned that Ethel's brother, David Greenglass, worked for the Manhattan Project, the U.S. effort to develop the atom bomb, they asked Julius to recruit him. He did. He also recruited another Manhattan Project engineer named Russell McNutt.

It was the discovery of another Russian spy that led to the unraveling of the Rosenberg network. A German physicist named Klaus Fuchs identified David Greenglass as a Russian spy. This discovery in turn led to the discovery of the work of Julius's spy ring. When Greenglass was arrested, he named Julius and Ethel as intermediaries with the Russians. The Rosenbergs were arrested in 1950, first Julius and then a month later Ethel. Their trial began in March of the following year. One of the young lawyers working for the prosecution was Roy Cohn. Cohn was a legal prodigy who had graduated from law school at Columbia at the age of twenty. At the time of the trial he was an assistant U.S. attorney. He was then twenty-four.

The tone and nature of the entire trial was clear from Judge Irving Kaufman's opening statement. He said, "The evidence will show that the loyalty and alliance of the Rosenbergs and Sobell [one of the members of their ring] were not to our country, but that it was to Communism. Communism in this country and Communism throughout the world. Sobell and Julius Rosenberg, classmates together in college, dedicated themselves to the cause of Communism. This love of Communism and the Soviet Union soon led them into a Soviet espionage ring." Months prior, the chairman of the U.S. Atomic Energy Commission, Gordon Dean, had said, "It looks as though Rosenberg is the kingpin of a very large ring, and if there is any way of breaking him by having the shadow of the death penalty hanging over him, we want to do it."

The case against the Rosenberg's turned heavily on the testimony of Greenglass, arrested the month before Julius. Initially, Greenglass indicated that while he had worked with Julius and passed information through him, to his recollection his sister, Ethel, was not involved. But later, shortly before the trial was to take place, Greenglass was apparently pressured into implicating Ethel in exchange for leniency for Greenglass's wife, allowing her to remain free and able to take care of their children. The attorney who interviewed Greenglass at the time and who handled his direct testimony implicating his sister was Roy Cohn. Prior to this point, the case against Ethel was seen as weak. But in the end, her brother's testimony would be her undoing.

While the Rosenbergs declined to answer many questions, pleading the Fifth Amendment, this was seen by the general public and those close to the case as tantamount to a guilty plea given the anti-Communist mood of the moment. On March 29, 1951, Julius and Ethel were convicted of conspiracy to commit espionage and sentenced to death. Sobell was given thirty years. Despite a massive public outcry against the execution of the Rosenbergs, on June 19, 1953, they were put to death in the electric chair at the Correctional Facility in Ossining, New York. Julius died with the first surge of electricity through his body. It took three to kill Ethel, and those in attendance said smoke rose from her head after she was finally pronounced dead.

In the years that followed, while Julius's role as a spy was confirmed again and again as new information came to light, questions remained about whether Ethel was actively involved as an agent, whether she helped prepare materials for the Soviets, or whether she was perhaps essentially a bystander, aware but not actively engaged. Sobell, in an interview with *The New York Times* in 2008, at the age of ninety-one, admitted the role he and Julius played (after denying it for years), but said of Ethel, "She knew what he was doing, but what was she guilty of? Of being Julius's wife."

It is also worth noting that subsequent revelations have not only raised questions about the treatment of Ethel, but they have suggested that whatever Julius and his associates did do, they probably did not give the Russians any information that materially aided their nuclear weapons program. Those aspects of their crimes, including the value of crude drawings of atomic weapons parts Greenglass was said to have passed along, also seem to have been much overstated in the trial and in the government's public condemnations of the Rosenbergs and their associates.

In the same article in which the late-in-life confession of Sobell was presented, the *Times* quotes historian Bruce Craig, who addressed the broader context of the conviction against Ethel, the coerced testimony, and other instances of dubious, fabricated, or overplayed evidence, saying that the case teaches "us what people will do to get a conviction. They took somebody who they basically felt was guilty and by hook or by crook they were going to get a jury to find him guilty."

At the center of this was Cohn, who would later become the mentor of Donald Trump and his prototype for what a "get it done" lawyer should be. (Cohn is often cited as precisely the kind of lawyer Trump was looking for when he appointed William Barr to be U.S. attorney general, a position Trump saw as primarily existing to protect him from his accusers.) One can only shudder at how things have changed and how, today, the same contempt for the law and for decency is being used by Cohn's protégé, Trump, to actually protect and defend his ties to Russia and to foreign interests and to reward and benefit the Russians for their military intelligence's attack on America's democratic institutions, an attack that had the express purpose of putting Trump into power.

Following the trial, J. Edgar Hoover personally recommended Cohn for his next job. Still twenty-four, he was appointed counsel to Wisconsin senator Joseph McCarthy (who picked Cohn over a young and too-eager Robert F. Kennedy). Over the years that would follow, Cohn would be instrumental in working with McCarthy to conduct further investigations into those who might be spying for the Soviets or sympathetic with their goals. This was, after all—and thanks to the likes of Mc-Carthy, Nixon, and Trump's mentor Cohn—a period when, hard as it may be to imagine today, being seen as having even the slightest association with America's enemies in Russia was the political kiss of death, instant and irrefutable proof of disloyalty to the United States.

The ugliness of the mood of that moment aside, it is also worth noting that, in fact, Russian spying was then as now and for all the years in between a real and deeply serious national security concern for the United States. That said, the fact that the Russians have been an active American adversary since at least 1945—three-quarters of a century—is also important in the context of Trump's choice of an overseas benefactor, their collaborative abuses and his subsequent defense of them, his willingness to invite future damage from them, and his desire to reward them for their systematic offense to elect him in 2016.

A NEVER-ENDING RUSSIAN INTELLIGENCE CAMPAIGN WAGED AGAINST THE UNITED STATES

There is little doubt that Julius Rosenberg betrayed his country. There is little doubt that in so doing he gave valuable information to a U.S. adversary that sought to use that information to build highly destructive weapons that had one primary purpose: to kill Americans, destroy American property, and defeat the United States. Yet, because the United States was not technically at war with the Soviet Union, indeed because they were an ally for much of the time Rosenberg and his ring were providing their valuable insights into the U.S. nuclear weapons program to their Soviet handlers, Rosenberg (and his wife and the members of their spy ring) could not be charged with treason. Given the narrowness of the constitutional definition of "treason" and court rulings that subsequently refined that definition further, the charge of treason was not levied in any of the most notorious cases of betrayal of the Cold War era—even though many did much more damage to Americans and American interests than in virtually any of the treason cases brought by the federal government in the history of the Republic. Lives were lost, secrets were transferred, weapons programs were compromised, strategic advantages were negated, our enemy was made stronger, and the United States was weakened, and yet it was not treason; it was called "espionage." And, it should be added, in a number of cases—such as that of Rosenberg collaborators like Russell McNutt—the absence of key pieces of evidence led to people who did great damage, by serving the interests of the government in the Kremlin, just walking away, unpunished—unpunished by the law, that is. Consistent with the premise of this book, history's judgment has been another matter altogether.

To give a flavor of the scope of Russian intelligence activities against the United States during the period between World War II and the GRU attack that took place prior to the 2016 elections, let us highlight a few of these cases of treachery, some of which involved some of the most notable names in the history of spying against our country. The list is far too long to include here, given the focus of our book, but it is essential to understanding the relentless nature of Russian intelligence efforts in the United States and thus the context, even in the wake of the fall of the USSR, for the recent campaign to help elect Trump (under the guidance of a Russian leader who was, of course, a senior KGB officer and veteran of the Cold War competition with the United States).

Among the most notable cases of the past fifty years or so

on behalf of the Soviets and their Russian successors are the following (in something like chronological order):

- In the autumn of 1967, Warrant Officer John Walker went to the Soviet embassy in Washington and began what would become a two-decade-long relationship. He stole documents from the navy, provided encryption codes for U.S. assets, and recruited his son, who was in the army, into doing the same. He did immense damage and may even have been responsible for the sinking of a submarine. Finally, his wife turned him in and the Department of Defense arrested him. The damage he did was enormous, and the benefits he provided the Soviets in terms of new technologies were equally great. His spent the rest of his life in prison for espionage. His motive was simple: he needed the cash.

- James Hall III spent the years from 1982 to 1985 assigned to a sensitive post in West Berlin. He was a signals intelligence officer and had access to everything from encryption codes to Soviet intercepts. Like Walker and his son, Hall was paid for this information by the Russians and provided it for approximately half a dozen years—until he bragged about his exploits to an undercover FBI agent. He spent almost the next quarter century in jail, having supplied the Russians with access to information that could have given them a critical advantage in the event of a ground war in Europe.

- Army Reserve Colonel George Trofimoff was the highest-ranking American ever convicted of spying.

He worked for the Russians from 1969 to 1994. He would steal documents—massive numbers of them—photograph them, and then pass them on to the Russians via a middleman, who happened to be both a Russian Orthodox priest and his brother. His brother went on to be archbishop of Vienna. Trofimoff was sentenced to life in prison in 2001.

- The spying went on, as we know, even after the fall of the Soviet Union. Harold J. Nicholson ran CIA officer training for two years in the 1990s. During that time, he sold the Russians vital information, identities, and assignments for all those trained during his tenure. He also shared secret information about the structure and staffing for the CIA operation in Moscow. He was apparently undaunted by his conviction and nearly twenty-four-year sentence for spying, because while in prison he enlisted his son to continue his work. He was convicted of espionage the first time in 1997 and then again in 2010.

- Robert Hanssen was a former cop from Chicago. He joined the FBI in 1976. Several years later he was working in counterintelligence when he sold information to the Russians about an undercover agent working within the GRU. After selling information to the GRU for another two years, he took a hiatus when his wife discovered what he was doing. His respite did not last long. By 1985, he began to work with the KGB, again providing information about U.S. agents working undercover in their midst. He took another break when the Soviet Union collapsed but reestablished contacts with the new Russian government in 1999. It was a fatal error. The FBI was aware there was a mole in their operation, and with the help of a KGB defector Hanssen got a taste of his own medicine. His crimes are considered among the most damaging by any spy of this era. It is believed that what he revealed to the Soviets resulted in multiple executions of U.S. assets. He was sentenced to life in prison after pleading guilty to fifteen counts of espionage and conspiracy.

- Aldrich Ames was a trusted employee within the CIA in 1985, over two decades after he had joined the agency. He spoke Russian, followed Russian intelligence matters, and then, as was the case for so many spies, sought to cash in on what he knew by offering to sell intelligence to the Russians for $50,000. Like Hanssen, Ames too revealed sensitive information about the names and missions of key FBI and CIA assets in the Soviet Union. After a series of these assets were arrested or killed, the U.S. government recognized that something was terribly wrong and they began an investigation that soon revealed that Ames had financial resources inconsistent with his government salary. Following a year-long investigation he was arrested, confessed, and was sentenced to life without parole.

Of course, many other instances of convictions for espionage and spying took place. These include spies for the Chinese, such as Indian American engineer Noshir Gowadia, who sold Beijing information on stealth technology; Chi Mak, a defense contractor trafficking sensitive technological information regarding the navy; and as far back as the Korean War, Larry Chin, a U.S. Army translator who gave the Chinese information that may have protracted that conflict—and then kept providing them with information until his arrest in 1985. It includes spying for allies, such as the work Jonathan Pollard did for the Israelis. It also includes the spying former Defense Intelligence Agency analyst Ana Montes did for the Cubans. (I once co-hosted a scenario exercise on Cuba at which one of the "expert" participants was Montes, then known to us only as a representative of the Defense Intelligence Agency.)

Naturally, during the "War on Terror" a new set of concerns was raised, and top priority was given to rooting out potentially dangerous extremists here in the United States or Americans who had gone to the Middle East to work for our enemies. Notable cases included that of John Walker Lindh, known as the "American Taliban," who was raised in Northern California, went to Afghanistan, worked alongside the Taliban, and then was captured by the United States three months after the September 11 attacks on the United States. Lindh said he had joined the Taliban because he believed in their form of Islam. While being tried he stated, "I have never understood jihad to mean anti-Americanism or terrorism. I condemn terrorism on every level, unequivocally." He was sentenced to twenty years in prison and served seventeen, released in May of 2019.

A different illustration of the kind of cases faced by the very different sort of war we have faced in trying to combat Islamic extremism is that of Anwar al-Awlaki. Born in New Mexico to Yemeni parents, al-Awlaki was raised partially in the United States and partially in Yemen. He attended Colorado State University and later also studied at San Diego State University in California and George Washington University in Washington, D.C. Active in Muslim organizations throughout his life, he became an imam and then was increasingly radicalized. He was seen to advocate for extremist causes, two of the 9/11 hijackers were known to have attended his sermons and later began working for an organization, the Charitable Society for Social Welfare, that was alleged by the FBI to be a front channeling funds to terrorists. Charismatic and a compelling speaker, he drew many followers and even led a service for Muslim congressional staffers. Minor run-ins with the law and growing suspicion of his role as a dangerous agitator led him to leave the United States in 2002, first traveling to the United Kingdom and then to Yemen. There he became deeply involved with al-Qaeda and served as a "senior recruiter," according to the FBI. In the wake of the shooting at Fort Hood in Texas by Nidal Malik Hasan, it was discovered that he was corresponding with al-Awlaki and viewed him as an inspiration or a mentor. It was also known that al-Awlaki had contacts with Umar Farouk Abdulmutallab, the so-called Underwear Bomber who tried to bring down Northwest Airlines Flight 253 in December 2009.

Because al-Awlaki claimed Yemeni citizenship and was a resident in Yemen, the U.S. administration of Barack Obama, having identified him as an "imminent threat," concluded that targeting him for killing would be legal under international law. This was complicated by his U.S. citizenship, and so any action would require the approval of the U.S. National Security Council. By early 2010, he was on a "targeting list" that was approved for action by President Obama personally. Cited as "extremely dangerous," he was added to the U.S. Treasury Department list of Specially Designated Global Terrorists by mid-July 2010. His father, a former senior Yemeni official and university president, launched an effort to have a lawsuit brought against the U.S. government with the goal of having his son taken off the list. A judge dismissed the lawsuit, saying al-Awlaki's father did not have standing and the Constitution had granted the right to conduct such military affairs to the executive branch rather than the judiciary.

One attempt to kill al-Awlaki by a missile fired from a drone failed. But by September 30, 2011, the White House acknowledged a car containing al-Awlaki had been destroyed in a drone attack. President Obama framed the death as a legitimate act of war against an enemy combatant, although international controversy was stirred by the action. Subsequent to this, al-Awlaki's son, brother-in-law, and, finally in 2017, his eight-year-old daughter were killed in attacks in Yemen.

A NEW ERA

The cases of treason, betrayal, espionage, and other forms of attack on the United States by those who arguably owed the country loyalty during the twentieth and twenty-first century reveal a broad diversity of circumstances, motives, and contexts. Some, as in past centuries, seemed unjustified. Some punishments were merciful. Some were cruel. Some were difficult to justify.

While many took place in the context of the great wars of the era, some took place under circumstances it seemed the founders did not imagine when they conceived the terms of the one crime so serious that they thought to include it in the Constitution—that of treason. Half of the twentieth century and all of the twenty-first have seen America face adversaries with whom we were not technically at war but who were intent on

doing us great damage. The acts of those who aided those adversaries were in every other respect "aiding and abetting" an
enemy, save for the government's failure to legally specify those
enemies as such with a formal declaration of war.

Some such acts were redefined as coming under the terms
of military justice. Others were prosecuted under different laws,
such as those associated with conspiracy against the United
States (familiar to those who followed Special Counsel Robert
Mueller's investigation, as we shall see in the next chapter) or
espionage. But still others defy description. They are not even
forms of warfare that the founders of the Republic could have
imagined.

Take cyber war or modern information warfare, for example: the damage that could be done by individuals like Edward
Snowden or Chelsea Manning by stealing data and making it
widely available on the internet, to say nothing of the data they
may have just directly provided our rivals and adversaries. Or
take the case of Russian military intelligence, which has been
waging operations in the United States for nearly a century,
doing massive damage to U.S. security, resulting in the loss of
lives and the endangering of millions upon millions of others.
It is undeniable that they benefited from the laws of the United
States that gave extra protections to our allies or undeclared adversaries. But now they also conduct their operations via means
that are hardly those of conventional warfare or espionage.

We now live in an era in which the idea of Cold War has
been succeeded by that of "cool war." It is neither the "hot"
wars we were accustomed to in the past, with industrial scale
destruction. Nor is it the Cold War of mutually assured destruction in which the cost of conflict was so high that nei-

ther side dared fight. Now we live in the age of cyber war, in which the risks to human life and infrastructure are—at least thus far—much lower than in other forms of modern warfare that have been more common in the recent past. It is hard to attribute blame for an attack. The targets are often not government but the private sector. Often the damage is the theft of information or the infiltration of infrastructure to enable more destructive attacks in the future. In the era of cool war, the cost of conflict is so low that for many actors the temptation is to never stop.

But we have no rules for such war. No doctrines. We don't know if a cyber attack amounts to real war or not. We don't have accepted doctrines as to whether it is reasonable to respond to a cyber attack with force. And in an era of constant shadow wars, there are no declarations of conflict. Indeed, it is one of the "advantages" of such conflict that no declaration need ever be made.

But if the nature of warfare has changed so much that it is never declared and that aiding and abetting a cyber attack can look much different from aiding and abetting a conventional attack (it might just be leaving assets unprotected or underprotected—much as Benedict Arnold might have hoped to do with the fort at West Point), then how do we protect ourselves against the worst of crimes against a nation?

Indeed, in the wake of the GRU attacks in 2016, we have actually learned that we are ill-prepared to deal with such crimes, that our laws are unsuited to ensure the safety of our institutions, that we have new and growing vulnerabilities. (This is not helped by having a government under Trump and McConnell that has seen fit to unfund or underfund efforts to protect from future such attacks—either as a continuing sign of their complicity or out of fear that successful such efforts might reconfirm that the Russian attacks in 2016 were real, serious, and part of a problem and not an element in a "witch hunt," as in the fantasy promoted by Trump.) We need to understand that and rethink its consequences. And one of the best ways we can demonstrate the urgency of that need is to examine exactly what happened during that campaign in 2016 and afterward. We need to understand how our enemies acted and whether or not it could be compared to past wars or acts of espionage. We need to understand how those who owed allegiance to the United States—including a man who sought the highest office in the land and later won and would occupy that office—acted in the face of such acts. Did he "adhere" to that enemy? Did he gave them aid and comfort? Did those around him? Or have they found a new way to work with our enemies to weaken us, a way for which there are no consequences?

Finally, especially in the context of this book, we must ask whether, quite apart from the technicalities of the law, past history suggests how these new sorts of crimes in this new age of warfare might be viewed by the ultimate court, that in which the presiding judge is time and the jury is the collective memory of men and women yet unborn. Today we can set aside juries and say that though Julius and Ethel Rosenberg received the same sentence, they should be remembered differently. Although Walter Allen was convicted of treason, we now realize that he, like John Brown, was more hero than villain. We have the perspective to realize that when the government is overzealous, it can be responsible for crimes even as it ostensibly seeks to prevent them. We have seen the cost of the abuse of government power and the undermining or circumventing of the rule of law. And we can ask, What if such approaches were used not to prosecute wrongdoers but to protect them?

These are the questions of the next chapter and the remainder of this book.

5

ADHERING TO OUR ENEMIES

Take it from someone who fled the Iron Curtain: I know what happens when you give the Russians a green light.

—Madeleine Albright

There is a danger in projecting how history will assess a presidency that is still in progress. Presidencies are often defined in moments, crises, or breakthroughs that can take place in days or weeks or just a few months. Most presidencies change in character over time as the president masters the job or ages, as his aides come and go, as the political makeup of the Congress and the country shifts.

We have all seen this phenomenon in our lifetimes. Nixon before and after Watergate could not have been more different. Jimmy Carter's presidency was irreversibly altered when American embassy personnel were taken hostage in Tehran. Reagan declined rapidly in his last few years as a result of his age or the aftereffects of the attempt on his life or the early symptoms of his Alzheimer's disease. The presidency of George H. W. Bush was brief but largely defined by a handful of major events that shaped his legacy: the Gulf War, the Tiananmen Square Massacre, and the fall of the USSR. Bill Clinton's impeachment in 1998 was clearly a major turning point in how he was and is perceived. While George W. Bush's presidency seemed likely to be defined by what happened in his first year in office in response to the September 11 attacks, the financial crisis that occurred in 2007 and 2008 again altered views of him dramatically. Barack Obama became substantially less conservative in his last year or two in office and accumulated major achievements like the Paris Accords and Trans-Pacific Partnership. And while first-term Obama would likely be judged primarily for his signature health-care legislation, by 2013 his uncertain handling of the Syria crisis also emerged as a legacy that would shape his reputation. Further on in each and every case, time has altered our impressions, downplaying some issues that seemed more significant at the time, emphasizing others, including some that were largely invisible as they transpired.

Having said that, in some instances, the character of presidencies and presidents may be revealed early, and yet, despite the ebb and flow of events during an administration, it is what in the end endures. For all the crises he faced, the hope engendered by the presidency of John F. Kennedy is, to many, his legacy. The same might said, despite the above-noted evolutions, for Ronald Reagan and for Barack Obama.

Thus, the same is true of the extraordinary case of Donald Trump and the Russian effort to help him win election in 2016. Quite apart from the fact that Trump has shown over his first term in office very little growth or evolution as a president, nor, indeed, has he shown any interest in achieving such growth, the Russian attack on American democracy and the fact that an

American candidate for president embraced it and then later, as president, defended it and rewarded it, is an event without precedent in twenty-four decades of U.S. history. Its import is underscored by the fact that it has had major lasting and sweeping consequences, including Trump's attacks on our allies; efforts to undermine international institutions created in the wake of World War II; Trump's gifting northern Syria to Russian control, even though it involved selling out our Kurdish allies; the special relationship forged between Trump and Putin; support for Russian initiatives in the United Nations and for Russia's return to the G8 (known prior to Russia's joining as the G7, the Group of Seven, the club of the world's most influential economies); and even the Ukraine scandal that really precipitated the congressional effort to impeach Trump, a scandal about withholding aid in a way that benefited Russia and sought an investigation into 2016 campaign that would have had the effect of exculpating Russia. (Indeed, the Ukraine scandal has proven to be merely an extension of the initial Russia case, involving an overlapping cast, similar motives, and the heavy hand of Vladimir Putin.)

To assess how future generations will judge Trump, those close to him, and their behavior during this period nonetheless requires caution. Trump himself is an inflammatory figure in a period in American history that is even more fraught than usual with tension and political polarization—which, as we have seen even in the brief descriptions of past events we have reviewed in this book, is saying quite a lot. It is easy to let emotion or partisanship cloud our views. Further, many of the facts of Trump's behavior and that of his relatives and close aides during this period are still unclear. For all the investigations concerning Trump and Russia, Trump and Ukraine, and Trump and his overseas financial ties, much remains unknown or subject to speculation. Some of those blank spots in our understanding are due to deliberate obfuscation, including by the White House, the attorney general, and even members of the U.S. Congress. Some are due to the fact that serious investigations into them are still ongoing and beyond the view of the public. Some are simply due to the complexity of the cases. Further, as the cases associated with Trump's willingness to trade favors with foreign governments who did favors for him fade into the past, they are overtaken by other events that color our perception of him as a leader, of how he prioritizes self-interest before public duty, as in the case of the Covid-19 outbreak.

In the interests of rigor and fairness, therefore, our approach to placing these events in a historical context will involve looking only at what we know for sure, at what is a matter of public record, either as a result of the work of Special Counsel Robert Mueller and his team, of congressional testimony in the impeachment case, of testimony in other legal cases, or as a result of well-established, reputable reporting confirmed in multiple news outlets. We will base our analysis on these facts alone and will address, once we're done, how existing, open questions might alter history's perception once they are answered.

That said, we must also recognize that some of our definitive sources have actually been very severely limited in the scope of their investigations and their ability to get to core facts—especially in the case of the Mueller Report and the other investigations colored by the actions of the Trump-Barr Justice Department. (Mueller himself laments his inability to get to key facts due to lack of White House cooperation, lying by witnesses, and other impediments. Perhaps someday soon we will also know what constraints were placed on him from above, by his supervisors within the Trump Department of Justice.) We will consider those limitations and define them for ourselves in a moment. But before we do, it is important to note that it is our assessment that enough is known, enough has been established and proven conclusively, enough has taken place in the public eye for us to draw confident conclusions about where the behavior of Trump and his team may fit in the long litany of betrayals that I have summarized in the previous chapters of this book. What has happened stands out from all we have already seen in certain important ways; and by understanding that and by sharing that understanding, how voters and public officials take actions that can impact Trump's future may well be affected. Indeed, it should be. Because it should already be clear that what happened in 2016 and since is in a class by itself in the history of great betrayals of America and the American people since 1776.

THE MUELLER REPORT: AN INCOMPLETE PICTURE OF EVENTS

The initial mandate to Robert Mueller at the time he was appointed as special counsel, according to the letter appointing him signed by Deputy Attorney General Rod Rosenstein, was to investigate

1. any links and/or coordination between the Russian government and individuals associated with the campaign of President Donald Trump;

2. any matters that arose or may arise directly from the investigation; and

3. any other matters within the scope of [the law].

That last point gave the special counsel "authority to investigate and prosecute federal crimes committed in the course of, and with intent to interfere with, the Special Counsel's investigation, such as perjury, obstruction of justice, destruction of evidence, and intimidation of witnesses." Subsequent memos clarifying the mission were also produced by Rosenstein. They indicated that the special counsel would investigate any potential criminal activity associated with former Trump campaign manager Paul Manafort and campaign aides Carter Page and George Papadopoulos and interactions they may have had with the Russian government. Mueller also was given authority to look into other allegations regarding Manafort, Papadopoulos, and former national security advisor Michael Flynn. In addition, authority was also granted to investigate activities of presidential advisor Roger Stone (another protégé of Roy Cohn), former deputy campaign manager and Republican National Committee (RNC) official Richard Gates, and Trump lawyer Michael Cohen. Mueller was also asked to look into whether Trump's first attorney general perjured himself during his confirmation process.

As has been repeated often by both sides in this matter, within those parameters the investigation appeared to be quite thorough. The Mueller staff included nineteen attorneys as well as a substantial support team including FBI agents, intelligence analysts, researchers, and other experts and support staff. The team was given access to results of investigations that took place prior to its formation, including counterintelligence information. In the course of its investigation Mueller and his team interviewed 500 witnesses, executed almost 500 search-and-seizure warrants, 230 orders for stored communications records, 50 orders for call-and-message tracing, and issued more than 2,800 subpoenas. They also made 13 requests to foreign governments under legal-assistance agreements seeking their help in the sharing of evidence.

The investigation commenced in May 2017 (following the firing of FBI Director James Comey by Trump for reasons believed to be associated with his unwillingness to make a "loyalty pledge" to Trump or to tamp down investigations into the Trump campaign). It concluded in March 2019 (weeks after the appointment of new Trump Attorney General William Barr).

Noting all this, it is important to acknowledge what the Mueller investigation did not cover, where its scope was constrained or appears to have been in some way limited. That is quite considerable, as should be apparent from the parameters laid out in the memos detailing the Mueller assignment as charged by Rosenstein, his supervisor throughout the investigation (due primarily to the fact that Attorney General Sessions recused himself from the Russia matter—much to Trump's never-ending chagrin). The efforts of Acting Attorney General Matthew Whitaker and, later, Attorney General Barr to shepherd the investigation to what in retrospect seems a too-speedy conclusion, to suppress some findings, and to distort others also suggest that Mueller was not at any point unfettered in his ability to pursue the underlying truth or, in the end, justice.

The limits on the special counsel included the following:

- The duration of the investigation: Mueller, for example, did not pursue direct testimony from the president of the United States, despite its centrality to the investigation, because it was his judgment, according to testimony he gave before the House Permanent Select Committee on Intelligence, that seeking that testimony would delay concluding the investigation. While some, such as respected legal scholar and former Acting Solicitor General Neal Katyal, have argued that Mueller felt the president's testimony was unnecessary because the evidence was strong enough to make a case against him for obstruction, this does not address why Mueller, seeking information on the ties between the Trump campaign and the Russians, would not have interviewed the central player in that story—especially since his knowledge of potential crimes was so central to the determination of whether or not crimes were committed. The president's legal team in both the Mueller case and the impeachment had a tactic of stonewalling investigators and throwing up legal obstacles to getting evidence that investigators in both cases said made it difficult to get at the truth. In both cases the decision was made to proceed rather than battle in the courts and both cases were weakened accordingly. In my view, given the gravity of the issues in question, more patience was in order. Furthermore, the success of the stalling tactic and the failure to embrace similarly aggressive countermeasures creates a dangerous precedent for future investigations.

- In the same vein, only one person in attendance at a significant meeting between the Trump campaign and representatives of the Russian government at Trump Tower in June 2016 was not interviewed. That was the president's eldest son, Donald Trump, Jr. While speculation is that he was not subpoenaed because his lawyers indicated he would plead the Fifth Amendment in the event he was brought before Mueller, this gap in the investigation also seems salient. There is no reason that he, a central player in the campaign, deserved this kid glove treatment. (He got this again during the impeachment hearings despite the fact that he was present at key moments—such as the 2018 dinner revealed by Rudy Giuliani associate Lev Parnas to have included President Trump's declaration that he wanted his aides to "get rid of" the U.S. ambassador to Ukraine, Marie Yovanovitch.)

- In addition, during his congressional testimony, Mueller indicated that he did not investigate the financial ties of President Trump with Russians or those associated with Russians beyond quite limited parameters. While this was identified by the White House as a "red line" issue for the president, that is certainly no reason why information that could explain Trump loyalties or leverage others might have had over the president and his family was not central to the investigation. Of all the oversights of Mueller's investigation, this is perhaps the most egregious given the extent of the president's international business ties, the fact that some of those ties have led to other legal cases, as with Trump's financing from Deutsche Bank, and the fact that subsequently there have been revelations that those close to Trump, such as his former National Security Advisor John Bolton, felt that Trump may have been giving favors to "autocrats" around the world to advance his personal rather than the national interests.

- Mueller's investigation was also concluded comparatively rapidly compared to comparable efforts. It lasted 674 days, under two years, compared, for example, to the four-year duration of the Kenneth Starr independent counsel investigation into the Clintons. It is a matter of record, as a result of the investigation, that Trump repeatedly tried to end it, including by seeking to fire Mueller. While unsuccessful in this respect under Sessions, it appeared that once Trump had a more pliable acting attorney general in place with Matthew Whitaker (who oversaw the interregnum between Sessions and Barr), pressure on Mueller grew, and once Barr was in place, it intensified further. It goes without saying that a shorter investigation is likely to produce less information.

- Some areas of potential investigation were dismissed or given, in the eyes of some experts, short shrift. One of these is the investigation into campaign finance violations, which Mueller indicates in the report was set aside because it was seen as difficult to prosecute (due to, it seems, the difficulty in valuing the aid provided by the Russians to Trump). U.S. law bans campaigns from receiving any kind of contributions of money or in-kind services of value from foreign nationals. According to Robert Bauer, former Obama White House counsel, Mueller "treats the campaign finance issues almost cursorily—one could say, superficially—even to the point of failing to identify and address all the applicable law. The results are an unconvincing decision to decline any prosecutions, and a major question about the enforcement of this law in 2020 and beyond."

- Perhaps the most famous gap in the Mueller Report is its failure to recommend prosecution for the crimes it does seem to indicate took place—notably those associated with the possibly ten counts of obstruction of justice that it describes. Mueller indicated that such a recommendation was precluded by a Department of Justice Office of Legal Counsel memorandum offering the opinion that a sitting president cannot be indicted. This view, presented most recently in a memo dating to the year 2000, asserts "The indictment or criminal prosecution of a sitting President would unconstitutionally undermine the capacity of the executive branch to perform its constitutionally assigned functions." This view has been assailed by an army of legal experts as being inaccurate. Harvard Law School professor Laurence Tribe described it to me as "Insupportable. It is just wrong." Georgetown University Law Center professor Paul Butler once elaborated saying "Even if, to use Trump's own example, he shot someone on Fifth Avenue, the only remedy [under this opinion] would be for the president to be impeached by the House, convicted and removed from office by the Senate, and only then prosecuted in criminal court." There is no question in my mind that the memo is wrong. But what is salient here is that by embracing its views, Mueller was relieved of the obligation to do what prosecutors do, and that is to make a charging decision, which, in and of itself, raises questions. Even if the evidence Mueller presented was compelling, he noted clearly that it did not exonerate the president and that he would have said so if it did, and he indicated that he felt the appropriate next step would be for the Congress to consider the matter as the Constitution requires it does with regard to "high crimes and misdemeanors."

Beyond the limits just mentioned is the fact that Mueller was viewing everything through the lens of criminal law. His mandate was not to assess whether a betrayal of the public trust took place or whether the president and his staff behaved morally or ethically. It was not to assess whether what was done was good or bad or reprehensible. It was not to suggest how history would judge Trump's behavior. It was only to assert whether specific laws were broken, and beyond, whether he could prove that they were broken beyond a reasonable doubt. That is not, it should be added, the standard required for impeachment in the House of Representatives or conviction in the Senate of the United States. It is not the standard that any of us will use in assessing how we feel about Trump's behavior.

IGNORING AN ASTONISHING QUID PRO QUO

Mueller's approach was not only artificially narrowed but it precludes the most important assessment that each of us must make and that future historians will assess—that of common sense and basic values. For example, while Mueller did not or could not under his view of the law determine whether the Russian theft of DNC and Clinton campaign emails or their distribution of those emails, or their disinformation campaign directed at tens of millions of Americans, or their pro-Trump campaign activities (including having someone in a Trump mask and a Santa costume walking around the streets of New York) had any significant "monetary value" (which is, on its face, preposterous), he also did not look at all at the other side of the Trump-Russia equation. That is, to borrow a term that later became more closely associated with the Ukraine-related charges at the center of the Trump impeachment, what was the "quid" Trump and company were actually offering the Russians for their "quo"?

Mueller might not have been able to quantify the dollar value of a hack (although the number of folks he indicted for being involved in that hack, times the time they spent on it, might have given another comparatively desultory prosecutor a good way to do the arithmetic). But if he tallied up what Trump was giving the Russians in return by assessing what he was offering them, which no other American president of the past three-quarters of a century would ever have considered giving them, then he might have understood just how great the value of the Russian efforts was perceived to be in the mind of Trump and those close to him.

What is the value of the policy shifts, such as lifted sanctions, that Trump aides like Michael Flynn were offering Russian ambassador Sergey Kislyak in the weeks following Trump's election? What is the value of the sanctions on Russian oligarchs that were actually lifted or waived? What is the value of the access Flynn accorded Kislyak—or that Trump offered him and Russian foreign minister Sergey Lavrov a few months later, on May 10, 2017, the day after he fired James Comey? Or the value of the sensitive Israeli intelligence Trump provided them with in that meeting? Or the value of letting them bring a Russian photographer into the meeting and having the Russians effectively handle the PR from the meeting after it was over (rather than the White House or American press who were excluded from the event)?

What is the value of Trump's attacks on NATO and our individual NATO allies? What is the value of his support for Brexit and the undermining of the European Union? (Weakening the Western Alliance was certainly the top foreign policy priority of Russian national security policy under Putin, as it was throughout the entire history of the Cold War.) What is the value of the access he gave Russian president Vladimir Putin? Of the many summits and phone calls he had with him? Of conducting those meetings alone and without U.S. translators? Of letting Putin control the record of those meetings, and of Putin having greater access to their secret contents than any elected official in the United States other than Trump? Of walking out of those meetings, as he did in Helsinki in 2018, and publicly accepting Putin's word about the Russian attacks on American democracy over those of his own intelligence agencies? (Think about that in the context of what we were reviewing in the last chapter. Think about the value to a former senior KGB operative of having an American president become the Russians' chief spokesperson while he was attacking the credibility of the U.S. intelligence and law-enforcement communities.)

What is the value of the defense Trump offered of Russia's seizure of Crimea and his argument that the people of Crimea viewed themselves as Russian rather than Ukrainian? What is the value of ceding control of the situation in Syria to the Russians? What is the value of giving a free pass to Russia's North Korean ally to increase their nuclear arsenal and test their nuclear missiles while cutting back on U.S.–South Korean joint exercises? What is the value of giving Russia a free pass for its violations of the Intermediate-Range Nuclear Forces (INF) Treaty by unilaterally pulling out of it? What is the value of having Trump representatives like Steve Bannon work with Russian-sponsored campaigns to promote ethnonationalist governments in the United Kingdom, France, Italy, Austria, Germany, Poland, and Hungary? What is the value of Trump arguing for Russian reinstatement in the G7 even though the act that triggered their exclusion—the invasion of Crimea—has not been reversed nor addressed in negotiations (and even though Russia is not one of the top seven industrialized economies—not close)?

What is the value of weakening America's standing in the world, which has come with Trump's bungled foreign policy, ignorance, narcissism, and boorish behavior? What is the value of the damage America has done to international institutions by going beyond attacking alliances to pulling out of the Paris Accords, the Iran nuclear deal (Joint Comprehensive Plan of Action), and the Trans-Pacific Partnership trade deal (in addition to having pulled out of the INF Treaty)? What is the value of the division that Trump's polarizing presidency has brought to the Russians, who, as we know, have been actively seeking such fractiousness and conflict since the 1920s?

What is the value to Russia of withholding aid to Ukraine, which it needed to defend itself from Russia? Of using withheld U.S.-aid dollars to coerce the Ukrainians into investigating conspiracy theories that, as former National Security Council senior director Fiona Hill famously observed, were conjured up by Russian intelligence in order to protect the Russians? Of instances like seeking Ukrainian assistance in discrediting former vice president Biden, in terms of further undermining America's standing and the perception of U.S. democracy as fair and a standard for the world?

What is the value to the Russian government of the obstruction of justice that helped protect them? What is the value of the decision by Trump and Mitch McConnell and GOP leaders not to protect the United States from future such attacks on our democracy, as in the case of the 2020 election, needs that they determined would go unmet and unfunded? What is the value of the efforts of Trump and Barr to not only quash investigations into Russian activities but to actually undertake investigations into the actions of those members of the FBI and the intelligence community who sought to protect the United States from Russian attack? How do you assess the chilling effect that will have on future efforts to protect the country?

What is the value of essentially providing a road map to the Russians and others for how to attack American democracy and to do so within the gray areas of U.S. law? To get away with gaming our elections? What more value might be added when the president of the United States says in the wake of the Mueller Report being published that if the Russians were to do it again, to offer more information that could help him win, he might take it?

Mueller may not have been able to quantify the value of passing along to the general public tens of thousands of DNC emails via WikiLeaks or DCLeaks—although in my view, he should have tried. After all, look at what lobbyists like Manafort get paid to achieve just a tiny fraction of those benefits to a client, such as the long list just enumerated. They get millions. Look at what Russia was willing to invest in these outcomes. Look at what other countries pay to influence outcomes in the United States. Look at what campaigns spend on gathering opposition research. There are, Mueller's conclusions aside, many, many ways to establish that what Trump got from the Russians was of massive, measurable value to his campaign and, as such, that it was at the very least a violation of U.S. campaign finance laws, apart from the deep betrayal of the United States that came from collaborating with a known enemy of the United States in such an effort.

That said, we may not know for some time, if ever, what Trump passed along to Putin in their private meetings or what others in his administration or those affiliated with his administration passed along. But we do know that no American president since the United States became an active player on the international stage would ever have done any of the things that Trump has done for the Russians. None. It is not even a close call.

In 1968, Richard Nixon used a Taiwanese back channel to encourage the South Vietnamese to stay away from the negotiating table during the last days of his presidential election contest with Hubert Humphrey, as a way of scuttling a peace plan that had been engineered by outgoing president Lyndon Johnson and that was helping Humphrey, Johnson's vice president, in the polls. Nixon's team sent a message to the South Vietnamese leadership that if they waited for him to be elected they would get a better deal. What Nixon did was illegal, and Johnson called it "treasonous," but it differed from Trump's dealings with the Russians in several key ways. First, the Russians were and are U.S. adversaries whose primary foreign policy objective for three-quarters of a century has been to undermine, weaken, or destroy the United States. Second, the scope of the benefits accruing to the Russians and the damage done to U.S. interests flowing from the Trump sellout to Russia is vastly greater than in the Nixon case. Third, Trump compounded this behavior by then seeking to do the same thing with Ukraine and China in the 2020 campaign cycle. Fourth, Trump obstructed justice to cover up his crimes and those of his associates.

Trump's collaboration with Russia and its aftermath strengthen our enemies. His actions weaken our allies. They weaken us. They make the world more dangerous. They cost American taxpayers more. And in the end, they might cost American lives by inviting future conflicts.

This may not have been the kind of assessment that Mueller felt he could have or should have made. That should be the subject of a separate assessment of Mueller, who in my view, was too compliant with the wishes of Trump's defenders in the GOP and not robust enough in his defense of the interests of the American people, our institutions, or our Constitution. But these are also all facts of the case, all actions that have taken place in the public eye, that are known to all and deniable by no one. They should play a central role in determining how we must view the actions that took place during the 2016 campaign and those that followed from them.

Each of these extraordinary, unprecedented, uncalled-for, and reckless actions is identical to having written the Russians a check. It is identical to having passed to the British the diagrams of the fortifications of West Point. It is identical to seeking to cut a deal with the British or the French or the Spanish to achieve personal gain at the expense of the country. It is identical to broadcasting propaganda about American enemies like the Axis Powers in World War II. Every betrayal has a transaction at its heart. The investigation that Robert Mueller launched into the greatest betrayal by an American of his country in our time did not even consider these facts in the way that it should. But already any clear-eyed objective assessment of what transpired must do what Mueller did not. And that assessment must take into account that this matter transcends the narrow confines of Mueller's mandate, the constraints placed on him explicitly or otherwise by his supervisors, or of the laws that Mueller was empowered to consider applying in this case.

NONETHELESS, THE MUELLER FINDINGS WERE DEVASTATING

At the heart of the findings of the first part of the Mueller Report lies a discussion laid out in volume 1.2 about the definition of the word "collusion." The report notes that this is a term that the investigators could not employ because it is neither in use in U.S. criminal code nor is it a meaningful term of art in the law. The report chose instead to focus on "conspiracy," which is the federal criminal equivalent or the closest thing that exists to one in the federal legal lexicon.

Another term used in the report and drawn from the original mandate empowering the U.S. Office of Special Counsel was "coordination," which was defined by the report as "an agreement—tacit or express—between the Trump Campaign and the Russian government on election interference." But the report goes further, again narrowing the definition of what might constitute a crime to require "more than the two parties taking actions that were informed by or responsible to the other's action or interests."

This is a bit like the legal equivalent of defining the eye of a needle through which any successful case must be required to pass. This is especially true in the example of a case involving a foreign intelligence service. That is because it is the objective of foreign intelligence operatives to wish not to be defined explicitly as representatives of a government. This leads to the use of cutouts and other representatives who can deny their association with the government even if they may dangle it as an incentive in meetings or communications—which in turn made it difficult to meet one of the key standards in the "conspiracy" definition above.

Further, while the language used states that an agreement between the Trump campaign and the Russians could be "tacit," that standard was clearly secondary, from the prosecutors perspective, as it is harder to prove. And of course, again, foreign agents tend to want not to make explicit agreements that could later prove damaging. So much of what is done is done on the deniable side of "tacit," which is the most difficult place to make a case beyond a reasonable doubt.

Nonetheless, it is undeniable that Mueller's investigation did produce a remarkable array of indictments and convictions that themselves describe what can be most charitably described as a deeply disturbing relationship between the Russian government and the Trump campaign. At the conclusion of the investigation, thirty-seven individuals and entities had been indicted, including thirteen Russians and three Russian entities. Twelve Russian intelligence officers were charged by name. A Saint Petersburg troll farm was exposed and its employees charged for their information-warfare efforts. Seven guilty pleas or convictions were obtained during the course of the investigation, including from the president's former campaign manager, Paul Manafort; his former deputy campaign manager, Richard Gates; his former national security advisor, Michael Flynn; and his former attorney, Michael Cohen. Mueller referred fourteen possible cases of criminal behavior that fell outside his perceived jurisdiction to other offices within the Justice Department.

While the Mueller Report sought to set aside the use of the term "collusion," the facts presented within it made a compelling case that collusion did indeed take place—lots and lots of it—including over 272 contacts between Trump team members and Russia-linked individuals, in almost forty meetings. Further, as noted by The Moscow Project's researchers, "We know that at least 33 high-ranking campaign officials and Trump advisers were aware of contacts with Russia-linked operatives during the campaign and transition, including Trump himself. None of these contacts were ever reported to the proper authorities. Instead, *the Trump team tried to cover up every single one of them.*"

Indeed, despite the Trump administration's repeated claims that they cooperated fully with the investigation, they did not. This led former U.S. attorney Barbara McQuade to ask in a column for the Just Security website, "Would an investigation free from obstruction have established evidence sufficient for criminal conspiracy charges?" She concludes that in fact we can never know the answer, because as the Mueller Report and independent researchers like The Moscow Project have demonstrated, the White House and its representatives were consistently, systematically uncooperative with Mueller. "Mueller wrote about numerous instances in which witnesses lied or withheld information, deleted communications and used encrypted messaging applications," continued McQuade in her column. "Other practical obstacles prevented Mueller from completing his investigation, including some witnesses' refusal to answer questions on the basis of their Fifth Amendment privilege against self-incrimination, other legal privileges and the inability to obtain evidence located overseas."

She goes on to note, "the Mueller Report states that in light of these 'identified gaps,' in the evidence, 'the Office cannot rule out the possibility that the unavailable information would shed additional light on (or cast in new light) the events described in the report.' That is, **the obstruction may have worked.**" We will consider the facts associated with obstruction of justice later. For now, it is simply worth noting that the Mueller Report describes a deep relationship between Russia and Trump despite the obstacles he faced, that the obstacles were designed to hide behavior and actions, and so it is reasonable to ask "Why?"; note also that the behavior was systematic and continues to this day. (Note: I do a regular weekly podcast with one of the co-editors of Just Security, Ryan Goodman, a professor at NYU Law School, and have included other Just Security staff and contributors, such as Barbara McQuade, on that podcast from time to time.)

That deep relationship took several forms. First, one of the great and truly remarkable achievements of the Mueller Report was reflected in the detailed indictments he brought against Russian military intelligence (GRU) and the previously mentioned Saint Petersburg entities involved in the disinformation campaign: the Internet Research Agency LLC (IRA), Concord Management and Consulting LLC, and Concord Catering—all funded and controlled by close Putin ally Yevgeniy Viktorovich Prigozhin.

Mueller goes into great detail describing how these entities were engaged in so-called active measures—a term of art describing the efforts of intelligence agencies to influence international events. In the indictment against the Prigozhin-related entities, he describes how they sought to use social media to influence U.S. public opinion in favor of the presidential campaign of Donald Trump and against that of Hillary Clinton. This is an important point, underscored in the Mueller Report: almost all of the activities of the Russian government were designed to help Trump and harm Clinton. And the activities were considerable, including over thirty-five hundred Facebook ads and posts reaching more than 29 million Americans and perhaps as many as 126 million of us. The IRA also was actively involved on the ground in the United States during the campaign, attending events, organizing others, and recruiting Americans to assist its members. Key Trump advisors reinforced IRA messages by retweeting them or otherwise sharing them—although it has not been established whether they knew they were supporting a Russian effort or not.

While this was going on, the Russian intelligence service,

the Main Directorate of the General Staff (GRU) were complementing the disinformation campaign with hacking and dumping efforts targeting the Clinton campaign and the Democratic Party. These attacks began in March 2016 and continued for months. The GRU hackers employed so-called spear-phishing techniques in which they would send emails to targeted individuals inside key networks, baiting those individuals to click on links within the emails and thus "invite in" malware that could make its way through the networks gathering stored information, recording keystrokes, and essentially providing troves of data that could be mined and shared.

I was inadvertently made aware of this campaign when, during my time as CEO and editor in chief of *Foreign Policy* magazine, we received a heads-up from the federal government that we had been targeted, as had several other influential organizations. Fortunately, my team at *FP* did not fall for the phishing bait. But John Podesta, Clinton campaign chairman, and others at the Democratic National Committee and the Democratic Congressional Campaign Committee were not so lucky. The result was gaining access to scores of computers and tens of thousands of documents that were shared via a GRU-created website called DCLeaks via a blog created by a fictional persona using the name Guccifer 2.0 and, ultimately via WikiLeaks.

WikiLeaks dumped twenty thousand documents three days before the Democratic Convention as a way of creating controversy. Fifty thousand documents from Podesta's personal account followed over the next few weeks. It was clear to all who was behind this. That included Donald Trump. On July 26 of 2016, he brashly reached out to them for help finding emails that were reportedly missing from a personal computer on which Hillary Clinton stored some official correspondence from her time as U.S. secretary of state: "Russia, if you're listening, I hope you're able to find the thirty thousand emails that are missing." As noted by Mueller, just five hours later the GRU was at work trying to collect those emails as well.

According to volume 1, section 5 of the Mueller Report, conversations about the Clinton emails were taking place at the highest level of the campaign; among those involved were Trump, Manafort, Gates, and Cohen. But the actions of the campaign took place at multiple levels. Jerome Corsi, Ted Malloch, and other representatives of the campaign sought to coax WikiLeaks into further releases to damage Clinton in the homestretch of the campaign. (Roger Stone, whose trial was pending at the time of the release of the Mueller Report, was part of this effort, as we know from other sources.). When on October 7, 2016, the *Access Hollywood* video was released, revealing offensive comments Trump made about his predatory behavior toward women, it was followed within an hour by another dump of Podesta emails as a distraction.

Also noted in this section of report is the fact that WikiLeaks communicated with Donald Trump, Jr., giving him information about the launch of a potential anti-Trump website. WikiLeaks also encouraged Trump Jr. to ask his dad to mention it and the work it was doing. Trump Jr. tweeted out the link. According to PolitiFact, Trump mentioned WikiLeaks—in a very favorable light—164 times between October 10 and November 8 of the campaign, including, on October 10, saying, "I love WikiLeaks." WikiLeaks was widely known at that time—and it has subsequently been conclusively established to be a front organization used by the Russian government as a conduit for its disinformation campaigns, as well as a distributor for hacked content acquired by its intelligence agencies.

As a consequence, it was possible for Mueller to conclude categorically that the Trump campaign maintained an interest in the work of the Russian government throughout the campaign and was eager to use Russian resources to help collect and distribute information damaging to Clinton. (Prior to the Trump Tower meeting Donald Trump, Jr., was offered documents that would "incriminate Hillary and her dealings with Russia and would be very useful to your father. This is obviously very high level and sensitive information but is part of Russia and its government's support for Mr. Trump." Trump Jr.'s response was, "If it's what you say I love it especially later in the summer."

In section 9 of volume 1 of the Mueller Report it describes the Trump Tower meeting of Trump Jr., Manafort, Jared Kushner, an intermediary, and four Russians to discuss the information. The Mueller findings describe that the meeting was actively discussed at the highest level of the campaign, and Michael Cohen maintained that Donald Trump, Jr., had even mentioned the meeting with his father. The meeting focused on providing the damaging information Trump Jr. had been promised. While there was general disappointment at the level of the information promised, the meeting was nonetheless considered sensitive enough that Trump and his son worked to develop a story suggesting the meeting had another purpose altogether (concerning the repeal of Magnitsky Act–related sanctions).

In addition to contacts pertaining to the campaign, Mueller studied in a limited way other Trump ties to the Russians. Specifically, he detailed efforts to complete a deal for a major real estate project in Moscow that Trump and his organization sought to complete by finding Russian partners and winning the support of the Putin government. Efforts to begin this project started around the time the Trump Organization oversaw the presentation of the Miss Universe pageant in Moscow in 2013. In the years that followed, Michael Cohen, Felix Sater, and other Trump Organization representatives worked to hammer out terms, concluding a letter of intent in the fall of 2015. The day after this agreement was concluded, Sater emailed Cohen: "Buddy our boy can become President of the USA and we can engineer it. I will get all of Putin's team to buy in on this, I will manage this process. . . ."

In the wake of the signing, the Mueller Report describes outreach from the wife of a Russian energy executive (which implies closeness to the government) who offered help with the Trump campaign. This individual offered "political synergy" to the campaign. There was considerable discussion about how to pursue this, but in the end Cohen did not follow up. He did, however, make other outreaches to try to connect Trump directly with Putin. The campaign later denied that Trump's interest in the deal extended beyond the beginning of the campaign, but it subsequently turned out that the project—which would have brought millions of dollars of much-needed cash into the Trump Organization—was discussed not only throughout the campaign but after Trump was elected president. Cohen at first denied that Trump knew anything about this but later admitted that he had discussed the project and the idea of a Trump trip to Moscow with Trump and that Trump was intrigued. Scheduling difficulties made the trip impossible, but it is clearly salient that the Russians throughout the campaign were offering Trump something that he wanted. Cohen later pleaded guilty to making false statements about this project (the denials), but prosecutors sought leniency for him because of his cooperation with their effort.

Mueller also detailed the activities of Manafort, Gates,

Papadopoulos, Flynn, and Page with regard to senior Russian businesspeople and purported representatives of the Russian government. In each case, it was clear that not only were there links but that the parties involved repeatedly sought to lie about them and to misrepresent their actions. The report also describes contacts between Russians and top Trump administration officials and associates, including national security official J. D. Gordon, Attorney General Jeff Sessions, Jared Kushner, communications aide Hope Hicks, businessman and brother of Secretary of Education Betsy DeVos, Erik Prince, Kushner's friend Rick Gerson, and academic Dimitri Simes (who advised Kushner).

THE OTHER "QUID PRO QUO"

Much as "collusion" was a term carefully selected by Trump supporters to reduce the core of the Russia case to the search for something that was very difficult to prove and that, indeed, the Russian government and Trump had gone to great lengths to hide, a similar tactic was used in what might be seen as part 2 of the Russia case: the effort by Trump and his allies to coerce the Ukrainian government into both digging up dirt on former vice president Joe Biden and his son Hunter and to explore further a completely discredited conspiracy theory that the Ukrainians, not the Russians, were behind the hacking of DNC computers in 2016. The term the president's defenders settled on in their effort to mount a Ukraine defense was "quid pro quo." The president and those around him argued—ultimately in vain, given the weight of the evidence provided in testimony and by the White House itself in the form of its summary of Trump's July 25, 2019, call with Ukrainian President Zelensky—that while Trump may have sought to pressure the Ukrainians, there was nothing wrong because they did not explicitly say to Zelensky or his team, "Either you do what we say or you won't get the aid."

By the fall of 2019, after a whistle-blower had brought this case to the attention of the U.S. Congress, it became clear that this defense was not going to work, because so many people in and around the case felt that, indeed, there was such a quid pro quo. The Trump team then began to argue that if that was the case, it was benign and totally within the prerogatives of the president as the author of U.S. foreign policy to determine to use such pressure to advance U.S. interests as he and he alone defined them.

The House of Representatives of the United States began the second high-profile investigation into a Trump administration Russia-related, seeking-foreign-assistance-to-win-an-election-related scandal during his first term in office. It is worth noting that for largely political considerations—an inherent fear of focusing too much on an impeachment inquiry on the part of a group of moderate Democrats led by powerful House Speaker Nancy Pelosi—the House investigations, led by House Permanent Select Committee on Intelligence Chairman Adam Schiff, had a tiny fraction of the resources available to Robert Mueller. They had almost no dedicated staff and, as was quickly discovered, the House lacked (or was disinclined to use) any real power in compelling witnesses to testify via subpoena. While they did issue some subpoenas, these were fought by the Trump administration, and as of this writing remain unresolved in the courts. Further, issuing subpoenas had the unfortunate effect of revealing how little leverage the House had in enforcing them. Normally, failure to comply with such a subpoena would result in a referral to the Justice Department for enforcement. But in the era of Bill Barr, an attorney general determined to act more like the president's personal lawyer, there was little appetite in the DoJ to prosecute offenders from the White House or other executive agencies. The House technically had the right to directly penalize those who did not comply but hesitated to do this because it would have been both inflammatory and, again, likely contested in the courts. Thus, once again, the stonewalling tactic from the Trump White House had the desired effect of dissuading the House impeachment investigators from issuing many such subpoenas.

Nonetheless, this investigation quickly produced many reports corroborating the whistle-blower's assertion that Trump was seeking to use U.S. foreign aid as a lever by which to advance his own personal political interests. As it happened, he did this over a period of many months, beginning in the spring of 2019, both via the work of his attorney Rudolph Giuliani, the former New York mayor, and via the work of handpicked representatives in the government, including donor-turned-ambassador to the EU Gordon Sondland, Secretary of State Mike Pompeo, Attorney General Barr, and Vice President Mike Pence. Giuliani turned to disgraced, convicted felon and former Trump campaign chairman Paul Manafort for assistance in the early stages of the effort and, as documents subsequently revealed, was instrumental in promoting some of the Russia-backed conspiracy theories that Trump wanted the Ukrainians to investigate. Giuliani's colleagues Lev Parnas and Igor Fruman also played an active role in the case, and when both were indicted on campaign-finance-related charges, Parnas became a source of insights and more evidence of Trump's intent and the way the Trump administration sought to shake down the Ukraine president, seeking an announcement of investigations into the activities of Joe Biden and his son Hunter in the Burisma energy company and into Ukraine's involvement in 2016 election interference in exchange for the release of nearly $400 million in aid committed to Ukraine by a bipartisan vote of the U.S. Congress and an Oval Office meeting between Ukraine's president Volodymyr Zelensky and Trump. Not to be lost in all of this, as mentioned earlier, was the fact that Trump's decision to withhold aid from Ukraine not only provided him useful leverage, but it also benefited the Russians, whose ongoing incursion into Eastern Ukraine was the single greatest threat to the stability of Ukraine, an important U.S. ally.

This investigation—featuring hearings by the House Permanent Select Committee on Intelligence and the House Judiciary Committee—ultimately resulted in the impeachment of Donald Trump. The Senate trial that followed featured additional revelations that emerged after the House proceedings had concluded, including some from Parnas, as noted above, and the assertion attributed to former Trump national security advisor John Bolton that he was told by Trump that the president ordered the hold on aid to Ukraine until the investigations were announced. This was the most powerful firsthand evidence of Trump's intent in the case. Taken with the testimony of witnesses from the House hearings and the meticulously presented case of House impeachment managers led by California's Representative Adam Schiff, this compellingly rounded out the case supporting the two articles of impeachment brought by the House of Representatives—one for abuse of power and a second for obstruction of Congress.

While in the end, Trump was acquitted along party lines by the Senate, the record of the president placing his personal interests ahead of those of the national security of the United States was presented in a way that seems likely, as was in the

case of past impeached but acquitted presidents Andrew Johnson and Bill Clinton to shape the public views of the man and
the failings of his tenure for posterity.

SELLING OUT AMERICA

In the next chapters of this book, we will examine how Trump's
betrayals of the public trust—either through undermining the
rule of law (including notably via obstruction of justice), abuse
of power, or outright corruption compare with past instances in
American history in which presidents were compromised. Specifically, we will consider the cases of the only three other presidents ever to seriously face the threat of impeachment: Andrew
Johnson, Richard Nixon, and Bill Clinton. In addition, we will
discuss the cases of several past scandals that rocked presidencies, including the Teapot Dome Scandal during the Harding
administration, and the Iran-Contra Affair during the Reagan
administration. In so doing, we will gain a better sense of how
the manifold abuses of Trump that go beyond Trump-Russia
"collusion" and the benefits it brought both Trump and the Russians compare to those prior eras. That will be necessary to place
the entirety of Trump's betrayals—Trump-Russia collusion, obstruction, abuse of power, federal election-law violations, violations of the Constitution's emoluments clause, and other forms
of corruption—more accurately in a historical context.

But thus far we have been exposed to enough of our history
of particular kinds of betrayals—of treason and traitorousness
and selling America out to foreign powers or to others who were
considered a threat to our system of government—to place the
core of the Trump-Russia scandal in perspective. Even given all
the limitations on what we know to date about how the Trump
campaign and the Russian government worked in parallel and

together to help elect Donald Trump as the forty-fifth president of the United States, we have enough facts to understand just how extraordinary these recent events have been and where they fit in the rogues gallery of those who have done the country wrong. (Especially we know that the more evidence that comes out, the more serious the crimes it is likely to reveal, as the Trump team has over the past three years had every incentive and opportunity to make known any and all exculpatory facts they might have.)

When we compare what has happened under Trump, both in terms of the degree of the betrayal and its potential costs to date, not to speak of those that may be yet to come, it is clear that Trump lives up to, in one dubious area at least, his own vision of himself as larger-than-life. As a traitor, he is in a class by himself.

None of those who, in the entire course of our history, have been accused of treason, espionage, or other forms of extreme disloyalty to the United States rival Trump in a range of key respects.

None has been so senior in our government. Aaron Burr ran for the presidency and achieved the vice presidency, so he comes the closest. Jefferson Davis was a cabinet secretary. But both did not commit their betrayals until later, when they were in different capacities. Burr murdered a man as vice president, a great man at that, but that is not a crime against the entire nation in the way that Trump's betrayal is.

None has benefited so greatly from his own treachery, rising to the presidency of the United States, as Trump has done.

None has ever done anything to reward a foreign master to the degree that Trump has benefited his Russian partners. I enumerated earlier in this chapter the ways that they benefited.

Neither France in the case of Edmund Randolph, nor Spain in the case of Wilkinson or Burr, nor Germany in the case of the Haupts, nor the Soviets in the case of the Rosenbergs, nor any of their other agents reaped benefits like Putin has as a consequence of his investment in Trump.

None has ever embraced an enemy so vilified for so long. The Cold War may be over. But Russia has defined itself as America's principal adversary in the world, even after its defeat in that conflict. Russia and before that the Soviet Union has been America's most notorious rival for every year of Donald Trump's life. (He was born in 1946, the first full year of the Cold War.)

It remains to be seen what the lasting damage of Trump's betrayal will be. The war joined against the Union by Davis and the Confederates cost 620,000 lives and shook the foundations of the American Republic to within an inch of its endurance. But it survived. It is as yet unclear whether Trump will do more damage than he has done to America's standing, to our alliances, to our allies, to our economy, to our society, to our environment, or to the institutions of our government. It is impossible to quantify exactly to what degree Trump's partnership with America's most pernicious rival helped him win the highest office in the land. But with his margin of electoral victory in the three key states that tipped the Electoral College vote to him at only 77,744 votes—and with significant Russian resources targeting those states—it is reasonable to conclude that it was a factor in his victory. In fact, recent analyses suggest it may even have been a *significant* factor. For example, Damian Ruck, a researcher at the University of Tennessee–Knoxville, which conducted a Defense Department–funded study of the impact of Russian social media activity on the campaign, said their research indicated that for every twenty-five thousand retweets from Internet Research Agency accounts, a 1 percent bump in Trump polling was predicted. Is that conclusive regarding the final election results? Ruck said, "The answer is that we still don't know, but we can't rule it out." Speaking about the impact on the three swing states, he said, "It is a prospect that should be taken seriously."

An analysis by the website FiveThirtyEight of the impact WikiLeaks had on the campaign suggested it, too, produced results. Harry Enten, writing about the analysis, noted that in the month before the election there was roughly twice as much search activity pertaining to WikiLeaks as to, for example, the FBI. This may have helped Trump offset bad publicity (for the *Access Hollywood* video) and close the 7 percent polling gap between him and Clinton that existed a month before the vote. As Enten wrote, "Trump, for instance, won among voters who decided who to vote for in October 51 percent to 37 percent." As it happened, this was the period that Mueller noted Trump mentioned WikiLeaks over 160 times. In other words, he was helping to guide traffic to them knowing they were helping to drive voters to him.

As we know, some of those accused of treason or similar crimes by the United States in our history were more heroes than villains. And some were doing so out of a sense of principle or competing loyalty, no matter how warped. Trump was acting in his narrow self-interest. Despite understanding America's relationship with Russia, despite knowing that Russian intervention was wrong enough for him to lie about it repeatedly, despite everything, Donald Trump went ahead because he thought it would help him win, and if it didn't, it might help him advance his big project in Moscow on which he would make millions. Loyalty to the country did not matter to him. Duty did not matter to him.

What is more, in the wake of his victory, his behavior arguably went from bad to worse. He knew the Russian efforts were an attack on our democracy. He knew who was behind it because he was briefed on it by the leaders of our intelligence community. And his response was to attack that intelligence community, to deny what he knew to be true, to embrace, elevate, and reward his Russian benefactors and to continue to do so throughout his presidency. He, almost alone among senior U.S. officials, has maintained the stance that Russia may not have been behind the attacks. He has actively promoted the word of Vladimir Putin above those of his own handpicked intelligence and law-enforcement chiefs. He sought to quash investigations into the facts, knowing what they would reveal. He obstructed justice. He, working with Mitch McConnell and Bill Barr, left the door open for the Russians to do it again.

In other words he compounded wrongs with additional wrongs, near-crimes with real crimes, one form of betrayal with another, one vector of damage to America and our interests with another. And, as of this writing, he continues to do so.

For all these reasons, it is fair to assume that regardless of what conclusions Mueller may or may not have reached or been had been permitted to reach, regardless of what actions the Justice Department takes or does not take, regardless of whether the Congress of the United States impeaches Donald Trump or removes him from office, regardless of whether the American people do so even if Congress does not, we already know that Trump has not only earned himself a place among the ranks of those who committed the worst of crimes against the United States of America, but that he is high atop that list, among the worst of the worst.

Given that Trump remains in power and the threat of great

betrayals remains real, it is a chilling thought. One that perhaps motivates us to go back to basics, to the dictionary definition of what a traitor is, to a definition that puts such vile behavior in context. This is from the *Online Etymology Dictionary*:

> **traitor (n.)** c. 1200, "one who betrays a trust or duty," from Old French *traitor, traitre* "traitor, villain, deceiver" (11c., Modern French *traître*), from Latin *traditor* "betrayer," literally "one who delivers," agent noun from stem of *tradere* "deliver, hand over," from *trans-* "over" (see **trans-**) + *dare* "to give" (from PIE root ***do-** "to give"). Originally usually with a suggestion of Judas Iscariot; especially of one false to his allegiance to a sovereign, government, or cause from late 15c. Compare **treason**, **tradition**.

It is uncomfortable to admit the president of the United States is a traitor. But simply based on that definition and the facts now available to the public, it is impossible to deny it.

6

FRACTURED TRUST

The aim of every political constitution is, or ought to be, first to obtain for rulers men who possess most wisdom to discern, and most virtue to pursue, the common good of society; and in the next place, to take the most effectual precautions for keeping them virtuous whilst they continue to hold their public trust.

—James Madison

The Andrew Johnson who demanded retribution against traitors in the days after the Civil War is now remembered primarily for his defense of those traitors and many of their values. The Tennessean had been a Democrat, and whatever passions that may have been elicited in his heart by the Civil War, the Union victory, and the assassination conspiracy against Lincoln that nearly claimed Johnson's life as well, within three years a different man had emerged. Or perhaps it is more fair to say, the old Johnson, the one who had grown up poor in the South and immersed in the culture of slavery, the Democrat, may have returned.

He was once quoted as saying "This is a country for white men, and by God, as long as I am president, it shall be a government for white men." He was a racist. And the efforts in the Congress in the wake of the war to rebuild the South ran in the face of those beliefs. The year after the war did not see black Americans receiving the freedoms many in the North, especially the so-called Radical Republicans, and abolitionists like Charles Sumner had thought they were fighting for. National frustration with this, with the apparent aimlessness of rebuilding and the lawlessness that was seen across the South, led to a Republican victory in the Congress, and those Republicans made their priority the passage of the Reconstruction Acts of 1867.

These acts divided the South into five military districts under the command of military governors. This arrangement was to remain in place until state constitutions that were acceptable to the U.S. Congress could be drafted and approved. The vote was extended to all males, including freed blacks, but excluding former Confederate leaders, and this broader electorate was expected to participate in the process of redrafting the state constitutions. The constitutions would not be acceptable unless they enshrined in their terms the right of voting to all regardless of race. Finally, no state could be readmitted to the Union without ratifying the Fourteenth Amendment, which guaranteed all men equal protection under the law.

Johnson was vehemently opposed to these acts, and he dragged his feet on enforcing them, which in turn created deep tensions between him and the Republican members of his cabinet and the Republican leadership on Capitol Hill. As we saw earlier, he pardoned many former Confederates. He was public in his contempt for the radicals. Fearing that he would remove officials that did not share his viewpoint, the Congress passed the Tenure of Office Act. This act made it illegal for the president to remove without Senate approval anyone from a high office who had been confirmed by the Senate.

Johnson felt both the Reconstruction Acts and the Tenure of Office Act were unconstitutional. In a test of his view, he removed Secretary of War Edwin Stanton, the veteran of Lincoln's cabinet, widely respected for his management of Union military capabilities during the Civil War and an opponent of Johnson's leniency with Southerners. Stanton was also a supporter of the Reconstruction Acts and a favorite of the Republicans. Johnson replaced Stanton with another popular figure from the war, General Ulysses Grant. But the reaction from Congress was swift. They reversed the president's decision, and when they did, rather than challenge it further, Grant stepped down. It was a shrewd move on his part, enhancing even further his popularity, a fact that would be reflected the following year with his election as Johnson's successor as president.

Johnson, infuriated, relieved Stanton again (this time seeking to hand authority to Major General Lorenzo Thomas as interim secretary of war) on February 21, 1868. Stanton locked himself in his office and refused to go. Then, on February 24, three days later, the House of Representatives of the United States did something that had never before been done in U.S. history. It voted overwhelmingly to impeach Johnson. Impeachment efforts had been discussed throughout 1867, moves to impeach had been considered and rejected. But finally, the patience of the Congress ran out in the face of the Stanton matter.

Initially there were nine articles of impeachment brought against Johnson. Ultimately, there were eleven. All at their core are aimed at the illegality of Johnson's efforts to circumvent the Tenure of Office Act and ignored the powers conferred on the Congress by Article I of the Constitution. The tenth and eleventh articles of impeachment reflect the outrage of the Congress at the president's open disrespect for them. It is impossible not to read their words without thinking of the tenor of American political discourse during the Trump years.

Article X begins thus:

That said Andrew Johnson, President of the United States, unmindful of the high duties of his office and the dignity and proprieties thereof, and of the harmony and courtesies which ought to exist and be maintained between the executive and legislative branches of the Government of the United States, designing and intending to set aside the rightful authorities and powers of Congress, did attempt to bring into disgrace, ridicule, hatred, contempt and reproach, the Congress of the United States, and the several branches thereof, to impair and destroy the regard and respect of all the good people of the United States for the Congress and legislative power thereof, which all officers of the government ought inviolably to preserve and maintain, and to excite the odium and resentment of all good people of the United States against Congress and the laws by it duly and constitutionally enacted; and in pursuance of his said design and intent, openly and publicly and before divers assemblages of the citizens of the United States, convened in divers parts thereof, to meet and receive said Andrew Johnson as the Chief Magistrate of the United States, did, on the eighteenth day of August, in the year of our Lord one thousand eight hundred and sixty-six, and on divers other days and times, as well before as afterwards, make and declare, with a loud voice, certain intemperate, inflammatory and scandalous harangues, and therein utter loud threats and bitter menaces, as well against Congress as the laws of the United States duly enacted thereby, amid the cries, jeers and laughter of the multitudes then assembled *in hearing, which are set forth in the several specifications hereinafter written, in substance and effect.* [emphasis added]

The remainder of the article describes instances of the type described in the above language. Suffice it to say that it is both a distant echo of the words of Donald Trump and far more temperate and thoughtful than anything that typically crosses his lips or emanates from his Twitter account.

Article XI serves as a summary of the core points of the House's complaints against Johnson:

> *That the said Andrew Johnson, President of the United States, unmindful of the high duties of his office and of his oath of office, and in disregard of the Constitution and laws of the United States, did, heretofore, to wit: On the 18th day of August, 1866, at the city of Washington, and in the District of Columbia, by public speech, declare and affirm in substance, that the Thirty-ninth Congress of the United States was not a Congress of the United States authorized by the Constitution to exercise a legislative power under the same, but on the contrary, was a Congress of only part of the States, thereby denying and intending to deny, that the legislation of said Congress was valid or obligatory upon him, the said Andrew Johnson, except in so far as he saw fit to approve the same, and also thereby denying the power of the said Thirty-ninth*

Congress to propose amendments to the Constitution of the United States. And in pursuance of said declaration, the said Andrew Johnson, President of the United States, afterwards, to wit: On the 21st day of February 1868, at the city of Washington, D.C., did, unlawfully and in disregard of the requirements of the Constitution that he should take care that the laws be faithfully executed, attempt to prevent the execution of an act entitled "An act regulating the tenure of certain civil office," passed March 2, 1867, by unlawfully devising and contriving and attempting to devise and contrive means by which he should prevent Edwin M. Stanton from forthwith resuming the functions of the office of Secretary for the Department of War, notwithstanding the refusal of the Senate to concur in the suspension theretofore made by the said Andrew Johnson of said Edwin M. Stanton from said office of Secretary for the Department of War; and also by further unlawfully devising and contriving, and attempting to devise and contrive means then and there to prevent the execution of an act entitled "An act making appropriations for the support of the army for the fiscal year ending June 30, 1868, and for other purposes," approved March 20, 1867. And also to prevent the execution of an act entitled "An act to provide for the more efficient government of the Rebel States," passed March 2, 1867. Whereby the said Andrew Johnson, President of the United States, did then, to wit, on the 21st day of February, 1868, at the city of Washington, commit and was guilty of a high misdemeanor in office.

SCHULYER COLFAX, Speaker of the House of Representatives.

Attest: EDWARD McPHERSON, Clerk of the House of Representatives.

In the view of the House of Representatives, Johnson had ignored the Constitution and the will of the people and thereby violated the public trust. While among his high crimes and misdemeanors was his failure to follow the terms of a lawfully passed act of Congress, the greater crime was, as noted above, his failure to uphold his oath of office. In addition, his disrespect for the institution of the Congress was also considered an abuse of his power and a threat to the still-fragile institutions of the U.S. government. The vote to impeach was 126 to 47.

The trial of Johnson in the Senate was one of the greatest spectacles the capital had seen until that point. Tickets to the eleven-week-long event were difficult to come by, and the galleries were full. Johnson began to think he might lose his office and considered the ignominy that would follow. He began to backtrack. He appointed a new secretary of war, who was approved by the Republicans. Nonetheless, on the day of the vote to remove him from office, May 16, 1868, no one was sure what the outcome would be. The deciding vote was cast by Senator Edmund Ross of Kansas. Every expectation was that he would vote Johnson out—but he did not. Whether this was because he was concerned that Johnson would be replaced by a political rival of his, Benjamin Wade, the president pro tempore of the Senate, because he had been paid off by Johnson supporters (as some historians suggest), or whether he was, as former president John F. Kennedy suggested in his book *Profiles in Courage*, he simply voted his conscience, no one knows. But when he voted against the first article of impeachment, the handwriting was on the wall. Two more attempts also failed. Johnson survived the first impeachment attempt in U.S. history.

Johnson did not, however, win reelection later that year. In fact, although no president has ever been removed from office

by the Senate as part of the impeachment process, as we shall
see, none of the three who were impeached or nearly impeached
survived with either their reputations or the political fortunes
of their parties intact. Johnson was out in months, replaced by
Grant. Nixon would resign in disgrace, and the vice president
who stepped into his job, Gerald Ford, would not win election
in his own right. And Bill Clinton's hand-chosen successor,
Al Gore, would lose in the first election following Clinton's
impeachment—albeit in a very close contest. Thus we see that
the damage done by even commencing an impeachment hearing against a president is immense and lasting, more important in many ways in terms of the reputational and political toll
it takes than in any of the specifics of the hearings and trials
themselves. It's a fact rightfully raised by those who argue that
Donald Trump should be impeached even if it is unlikely the
Senate would vote to remove him from office. So far, the political
survival rate of impeachment hearings is zero.

THE GREATEST SCANDAL EVER. UNTIL NOW.

Each generation is both pleased and shocked by itself. Succes-
sive generations consider themselves to be living in the greatest
time known to man, because, the messiness of history aside,
progress tends to work that way, in a linear fashion, always
moving forward. But at the same time, few shocks tend to be as
great as whatever the present shock is, and that is why people
of so many different eras in American history have considered
themselves to be the most scarred by scandal, by top officials
taking advantage of their positions or failing to live up to the
responsibilities of their offices. And by money and sex.

We have already seen that even the founders were not im-
mune from this, with their era featuring every type of intrigue

and scandal—the affairs of Hamilton, Jefferson and Sally Hemings, even whispers about Washington. Even today those scandals resonate, as in the late summer of 2019, it was for the first time conclusively revealed that Aaron Burr had a family of color that he provided for but did not acknowledge. Men like Benedict Arnold and James Wilkinson schemed and scammed. Spies were everywhere. And major debates about whether officials were honoring the Constitution date back to the Constitution.

Subsequent eras had similar debates and scandals: the Petticoat Affair, a scandal centering on the morality of a young congressional wife, electrified Washington during the age of Andrew Jackson. But so did Jackson's dueling and his shady dealings in the past.

While Grant was seen as a potential white knight riding in to rescue the country from the debacle of the Johnson presidency, it was not long before friends of the Union general started to take advantage of him and sink his administration into a swampland of murky deals and compromising decisions. First, two big Wall Street financiers, Jay Gould and James Fisk, tried to corner the gold market. They felt they could cajole Grant into suspending U.S. Treasury releases of gold into the marketplace for long enough for them to cash in on their holdings. And just to be sure, they also sought to bribe administration officials and even Grant's friends and family members and pay off Treasury bureaucrats for inside information. The scheme very nearly worked. Once Grant was onto it, however, he took steps to block it and it unraveled. Later scandals involved a remarkable array of plain old kickback and bribery schemes that involved skimming from excise-tax revenues, selling the rights to western trading posts, and helping importers dodge payment of customs duties.

Grant was never personally at fault in any of these schemes, but to this day, his reputation as a president has suffered as a result of his failings as an administrator to maintain high ethical standards among his cabinet, close aides, and other senior officials. Perhaps this is unfair. Grant's accomplishments as a general and in helping the nation to recover from the Civil War were substantial. Further, the era in which he lived—like much of American history—saw the rich abuse their power and high-level relationships and play fast and loose with the law in order to make themselves even richer.

Some men ran to clean up the scandals, like Grover Cleveland. He, however, was soon embroiled in a scandal for having fathered a child out of wedlock, leading to the famous anti-Cleveland campaign chant, "Ma, Ma, where's my Pa? Gone to the White House, ha, ha, ha!"

Some others did better, notably Theodore Roosevelt and his effort to stand up to the trusts, the big consortiums of robber-baron businesses.

But periodically administrations would themselves be caught up in such scandals, as was the case with Grant. Perhaps the most notorious such scandals prior to the modern era occurred during the administration of Warren Harding. The most prominent of the scandals that afflicted Harding was called the Teapot Dome Scandal, after an area rich in oil reserves that was opened up to two oil companies in exchange for payoffs made to Secretary of the Interior Albert Fall. For good measure, Harding was also subject to a sex scandal. He used to walk in Washington via a tunnel beneath Lafayette Park from the White House to the Hay-Adams Hotel, where he would secretly meet with mistresses. One of them, Nan Britton, wrote a book about their relationship—and the daughter it produced.

NIXON'S THE ONE

Prior to the scandals of the Trump era, the greatest constitutional scandal in the history of the presidency took place from events stemming from the June 1972 break-in at Democratic National Committee headquarters at the Watergate Hotel by a group of five burglars, who, as it turned out, were on the payroll of the Republican National Committee. As the scandal spread, it became clear that they were acting as part of a secret program to help reelect President Richard Nixon by finding damaging information on his opponents. That this scandal was triggered by precisely the same kind of break-in that was undertaken by the Russians on Trump's behalf forty-four years later is either a grace note of history or a sign that dirty politics never changes. That said, it should also be noted that Nixon won the election in 1972 over Democrat George McGovern by a historic landslide. Unlike the Russian hack of the 2016 election, which almost certainly played some role in determining the outcome in the exceptionally close election that year, the Watergate break-in was completely unnecessary.

Worse than the crimes committed by the Watergate burglars was the subsequent effort by Nixon and his aides to cover them up. The course of that cover-up and investigations into the illegal activities of the Nixon administration took a massive toll on it. After the five burglars were convicted and sent to prison in January 1973, it became clear that too many people near to Nixon were involved. He forced the resignation of his chief of staff, H. R. Haldeman, his counselor John Ehrlichman, Attorney

General Richard Kleindienst, and his White House counsel John Dean to try to stem the spread of what Dean would call the "cancer growing on the presidency."

Weeks later, in May 1973, the Senate Select Committee on Presidential Campaign Activities opened hearings into the Watergate break-in. They were televised and they made for such riveting, hard-hitting viewing that I can attest to at least one high school student in New Jersey staying home from school to be able to watch them. Two days after the hearings opened, a special prosecutor was appointed to investigate the Watergate affair. His name was Archibald Cox. Throughout, pressure from the media, with many new revelations coming from *The Washington Post* led by the reporting team of Bob Woodward and Carl Bernstein, kept raising public awareness of the scandal and forcing political leaders from both parties to take it seriously. While partisan divisions remained, there was a sense that the matter required an objective, intensive inquiry. It was nothing like the situation today, where Mitch McConnell and the Republican leadership on Capitol Hill have essentially granted Donald Trump a free pass to break any law, violate any standard, and they will not hold him accountable. Similarly, some of Nixon's own appointees, notably at the Justice Department following the departure of his first two attorneys general for involvement in the crimes, placed their obligations to their oaths of office ahead of that of their obligation to Richard Nixon or the Republican Party. In many ways, the crimes involved were not as great as those of Trump, his associates, and the Russians, but the respect paid to the Constitution and the sanctity of our institutions was vastly greater.

Hearings throughout the summer of 1973 produced further revelations, including that Nixon had been secretly recording meetings in the Oval Office, and that therefore there might be records of senior officials conspiring. Immediately a demand was made by the Senate committee for the tapes, but Nixon refused to turn them over. He based his refusal on the doctrine of "executive privilege"—the idea that presidential conversations must be allowed to be kept private if the president is to be able to fulfill his constitutional responsibilities. A legal battle ensued and at the end of August a judge ordered the tapes to be turned over. Nixon refused, instead offering up his own edited version of the tapes.

Tensions built throughout that period, and Nixon sought to remove officials he felt were not sufficiently loyal to him or not doing enough to protect him. (Nixon, veteran of the House Un-American Activities Committee and the red scare, was also close to Roy Cohn, who was one of those who advised him to hang tough during this period.) Just as Trump sought to fire Mueller and also eliminated Attorney General Jeff Sessions for not adequately standing up for him (replacing him with Bill Barr), Nixon, on the evening of October 20, 1973, ordered the firing of Cox, the special prosecutor. His then attorney general, Elliot Richardson, refused to comply. Nixon demanded his resignation. Richardson's deputy, William Ruckelshaus, also refused to fire Cox. Nixon forced his resignation as well. Finally, Solicitor General Robert Bork fired Cox. Eleven days later Cox was replaced by another special prosecutor, Leon Jaworski. Unfortunately for Nixon, he, too, would take his oath to the Constitution more seriously than his loyalty to the increasingly desperate president.

On November 21, 1973, the White House revealed that there was an eighteen-minute gap on a key tape. The president's secretary accepted the blame. This did not placate anyone. The case concerning the tapes went to the Supreme Court. In its decision on the case, *United States v. Nixon,* the Court ruled that the president is not above the law and must comply with the subpoenas for the tapes. It is a case that will certainly have resonance in the face of repeated efforts by the Trump administration to ignore lawful subpoenas from the U.S. Congress.

The Court's ruling was on July 24, 1974. By July 27, the House Judiciary Committee approved three articles of impeachment against Nixon.

Those articles, like those against Andrew Johnson, underscore what precedent there is for the Congress to find a betrayal of the public trust so great that it amounts to high crimes and misdemeanors, justifying the removal of a president from his high office. Following a preamble framing the case, the three articles of impeachment break Nixon's wrongdoing into three categories. First, in Article I, the specifics regarding the break-in at the Watergate DNC headquarters are laid out. Nixon is accused of using "the powers of his high office" to personally and through the actions of his associates engage in or seek to conduct a cover-up to hide the truth about laws that were broken. Examples given, which resonate with today, include "making . . . false or misleading statements to lawfully authorized investigative officers," "withholding relevant and material evidence or information," "approving, condoning, acquiescing in, and counseling witnesses with respect to the giving of false or misleading statements," "interfering or endeavoring to interfere with the conduct of investigations by the Department of Justice . . . , the Federal Bureau of Investigation, . . . the Office of Watergate Special Prosecution Force, and Congressional Committees," "approving, condoning, and acquiescing in, the surreptitious payment of substantial sums of money for the purpose of obtaining the silence or influencing the testimony of witnesses," "endeavoring to misuse the Central Intelligence Agency," "disseminating information received from . . . the Department of Justice . . . to subjects of investigations," "making false or misleading public statements for the purpose of deceiving the people of the United States," and "endeavouring to cause prospective defendants, and individuals duly tried and convicted, to expect favored treatment and consideration in return for their silence or false testimony." Indeed, these charges do not simply resonate with charges made against the Trump administration; it appears that Trump used them as a road map for his administration's behavior in the Russia and Ukraine cases.

Article II focuses on ways that Nixon abused his power as president. It cites efforts to use IRS investigations as leverage or to penalize enemies, misusing the power and resources of the FBI and the Secret Service "for purposes unrelated to national security," his efforts through the White House "plumbers" unit to use campaign finances and elements of the U.S. government including the CIA to engage in "covert and unlawful activities" and to influence outcomes of trials, failing to "take care that the laws were faithfully executed by failing to act when he knew or had reason to know that his close subordinates endeavored to impede and frustrate lawful inquiries by duly constituted executive, judicial, and legislative entities," and in a charge that could also be used verbatim to refer to efforts by Trump and Barr to go after their perceived enemies associated with the Russia investigation, Article II's final numbered assertion reads:

> *In disregard of the rule of law, he knowingly misused the executive power by interfering with agencies of the executive branch, including the Federal Bureau of Investigation,*

the Criminal Division, and the Office of Watergate Special
Prosecution Force, of the Department of Justice, and the
Central Intelligence Agency, in violation of his duty to take
care that the laws be faithfully executed.

Article III also directly speaks to issues that are identical to the abuses by President Trump. It says that President Nixon

failed without lawful cause or excuse to produce papers and
things as directed by duly authorized subpoenas issued by
the Committee on the Judiciary of the House of Representa-
tives on April 11, 1974, May 15, 1974, May 30, 1974, and
June 24, 1974, and willfully disobeyed such subpoenas. The
subpoenaed papers and things were deemed necessary by
the Committee in order to resolve by direct evidence funda-
mental, factual questions relating to Presidential direction,
knowledge, or approval of actions demonstrated by other
evidence to be substantial grounds for impeachment of the
President. In refusing to produce these papers and things,
Richard M. Nixon, substituting his judgment as to what ma-
terials were necessary for the inquiry, interposed the powers
of the Presidency against the lawful subpoenas of the House
of Representatives, thereby assuming to himself functions
and judgments necessary to the exercise of the sole power of
impeachment vested by the Constitution in the House of Rep-
resentatives.

The House hearings at which these articles were voted on were, again, events that were, unlike the rancorous Johnson hearings or the partisan charade that led to the impeachment of Bill Clinton, reverential in their appreciation of the importance of what was being done. There was a sense that the American system of government was at stake and that partisanship needed to be set aside and greater priorities recognized.

No one at the time captured this as eloquently as Congresswoman Barbara Jordan of Texas. In one memorable statement during the hearings that took place, she said, after offering a few introductory courtesies,

> Earlier today we heard the beginning of the Preamble to the Constitution of the United States, "We, the People." It is a very eloquent beginning. But when that document was completed on the 17th of September in 1787, I was not included in that "We, the People." I felt somehow for many years that George Washington and Alexander Hamilton must have left me out by mistake. But through the process of amendment, interpretation, and court decision I have finally been included in "We, the People."
>
> Today I am an inquisitor. I believe hyperbole would not be fictional and would not overstate the solemnness that I feel right now. My faith in the Constitution is whole, it is complete, it is total. I am not going to sit here and be an idle spectator to the diminution, the subversion, the destruction of the Constitution.

Jordan's remarks underscored that despite the defects of the Constitution, the document was valuable to us because it contained the seeds of its own revision and reinvention, as well as those essential elements ensuring its preservation. The Judiciary Committee approved the articles on a bipartisan basis with the twenty-one Democratic members of the committee joined by at least seven GOP members on each of the three articles they approved. But then, before the full House could vote on impeachment, leaders of the Republican Party, led by Senator Barry Goldwater of Arizona, the dean of the conservatives in the House and the 1964 presidential nominee of the Republican Party, went to Nixon and said they could support him no longer, that he would likely lose a vote in the Senate, and that he must resign.

On August 8, 1974, Nixon spoke to the nation:

I have never been a quitter. To leave office before my term is completed is abhorrent to every instinct in my body. But as President, I must put the interest of America first. America needs a full-time President and a full-time Congress, particularly at this time with problems we face at home and abroad. To continue to fight through the months ahead for my personal vindication would almost totally absorb the time and attention of both the President and the Congress in a period when our entire focus should be on the great issues of peace abroad and prosperity without inflation at home. Therefore, I shall resign the Presidency effective at noon tomorrow.

Following Nixon's resignation, his successor, Gerald Ford, sought to end the country's "long national nightmare" by pardoning Nixon. While he did not face prosecution for any charges against him, subsequently Nixon's men, Attorney General Mitchell, Haldeman, and Ehrlichman were found guilty of obstruction of justice. Three years later, in a television interview, Nixon defended his actions with language that has become a template for Trump and Barr; he denies it was even possible for him to commit any crimes because, "I'm saying when the president does it, that means it is not illegal."

The scandal shook the country to the core. The presidencies of Gerald Ford, Jimmy Carter, and Ronald Reagan all had as their core messages a desire to help the country heal, to feel good about itself again. But that was a struggle both because of external events (energy crises, the Iranian hostage situation) and because of continuing modest scandals. In the middle of the term of Ronald Reagan, a more serious scandal took place that again put the White House in confrontation with the Congress. It centered on secret efforts by the White House to fund anti-Communist forces in Central America despite prohibitions on doing so from the Congress. An elaborate scheme was hatched to funnel money from Middle Eastern sources to Central America and then, when it came to light and the White House was questioned about it, White House officials lied. In the end, two White House national security advisors, Robert McFarlane and John Poindexter, were forced to step down, as were a host of others at the center of the scandal, including Marine Corps Lieutenant Colonel Oliver North, a member of the National Security Council staff who was at the center of the scandal. It was called Iran-Contra (the money flowed from Iranian sources to the "Contras" in Central America) and the result was a major restructuring of the National Security Council staff, which has impacted how that vital advisory and policy-implementation-and-oversight entity in the White House operates to this day.

THE MEANING OF THE WORD "IS"

There was one more instance in our history in which a president was impeached. In 1998, President Bill Clinton was charged by the Republican-led House of Representatives with one count of perjury and one count of obstruction of justice. Innocent as such charges might seem in the context of current events, the scandal did lead Clinton to face a fate even Nixon had not. On December 19, 1998, he was formally impeached by the House.

At the center of the scandal was an affair that Clinton had with a twenty-two-year-old White House intern named Monica Lewinsky. It was not much, even as presidential sex scandals go, but when Clinton testified about it he denied having sexual relations with Lewinsky, a fact that was later proven not to be true. Further, Clinton was found by the independent counsel assigned to investigate him to have also taken steps to try to deny the affair had taken place.

It should be noted that the independent counsel, Kenneth Starr, had been appointed in 1994 to investigate a series of accusations concerning Clinton. They ranged from questions about involvement by Clinton and his wife, Hillary, in a real estate investment scandal called Whitewater to questions about the misuse of FBI files. In the course of these investigations, the Lewinsky scandal broke, and Starr, who was perhaps the most highly partisan "independent prosecutor" that the country has seen, zeroed in on it as the only result of his four-year search for incriminating dirt on the president. (Starr would later appear on behalf of Trump's defense at his Senate trial.)

Clinton's behavior throughout was slippery at best. Nothing illustrated this quite so well as an exchange Clinton had during his grand jury testimony in which he was questioned on whether he had been truthful about having an ongoing relationship between him and Lewinsky. He responded in lawyerly words that will haunt him to his grave: "It depends upon what the meaning of the word 'is' is. If the—if he—if 'is' means is and never has been, that is not—that is one thing. If it means there is none, that was a completely true statement."

• • •

Two articles of impeachment against Clinton passed the Republican-controlled House of Representatives. The first addressed Clinton's lies under oath on the Lewinsky matter:

> *On August 17, 1998, William Jefferson Clinton swore to tell the truth, the whole truth, and nothing but the truth before a Federal grand jury of the United States. Contrary to that oath, William Jefferson Clinton willfully provided perjurious, false and misleading testimony to the grand jury.*

In this article, its GOP authors, many of whom sat in judgment of Trump, wrote of Clinton's lying that:

> *In doing this, William Jefferson Clinton has undermined the integrity of his office, has brought disrepute on the Presidency, has betrayed his trust as President, and has acted in a manner subversive of the rule of law and justice, to the manifest injury of the people of the United States.*
>
> *Wherefore, William Jefferson Clinton, by such conduct, warrants impeachment and trial, and removal from office and disqualification to hold and enjoy any office of honor, trust, or profit under the United States.*

The second article that passed stipulated:

> *In his conduct while President of the United States, William Jefferson Clinton, in violation of his constitutional oath faithfully to execute the office of President of the United States and, to the best of his ability, preserve, protect, and defend the Constitution of the United States, and in violation of his constitutional duty to take care that the laws be faithfully executed, has*

prevented, obstructed, and impeded the administration of jus-
tice, and has to that end engaged personally, and through his
subordinates and agents, in a course of conduct or scheme de-
signed to delay, impede, cover up, and conceal the existence of
evidence and testimony related to a Federal civil rights action
brought against him in a duly instituted judicial proceeding.

As in the case of Trump, these articles were approved on more or less a straight party-line vote.

Clinton's trial in the Senate began in January 1999. The Republican-controlled Senate failed to convict by the necessary two-thirds majority on February 12. There were fifty-five Republican senators and forty-five Democratic senators at the time of the vote. No Democrats voted to find Clinton guilty. But forty-five Republicans voted to find him guilty, and forty-five Democrats voted to find him not guilty. The remaining ten Republicans voted to find Clinton not guilty.

I served in the Clinton administration as deputy undersecretary of commerce for international trade policy and later as acting undersecretary of commerce for international trade. I was not a politically active person at the time—more of a policy wonk. Perhaps that is why the incident was so disappointing to me. The administration had achieved quite a lot during its two terms. The world was relatively peaceful. What crises arose were largely handled. The economy was booming; 23 million jobs were great. It was the greatest peacetime expansion in American history. The Cold War was over and America was the sole superpower in the world.

And Clinton presided over all of that.

He was not convicted of a crime. The work Starr did really did amount to a partisan witch hunt. Presumed scandal after presumed scandal led nowhere. Nonetheless, Bill Clinton was not, in Trump terms, "exonerated." Crimes or none, in the eyes of the public he was deemed to be sleazy and dishonest. Largely, I think, in retrospect, that is because he was sleazy and dishonest about certain aspects of his personal life. He had a pathological desire to be liked and loved, and it cost him dearly. But it not only cost him. Al Gore, running for president as Clinton's chosen successor, did not carry Clinton's home state of Arkansas in the 2000 election, a vital factor in a very close race. Hillary Clinton, despite all of her remarkable achievements and legitimate gifts as a public servant, was seen by a part of the country as being permanently vilified for her association with the record of her husband. Much of that was partisan and unfair and fanned by the flames of a new era in media and in scorched-earth politics. But much of it was also Clinton's fault and serves as a stark reminder once again, that the verdict of the court of public opinion can often be much harsher than that of prosecutors, courts, or impeachment authorities.

WHAT IF YOU COMBINED EVERY PRESIDENTIAL SCANDAL IN AMERICAN HISTORY INTO ONE?

While the crimes and scandals described in this chapter are spread across more than two centuries of American history, each of us, even the youngest among us, must feel a familiarity with them, as we have seen their like in just the past few years. All these abuses of the public trust have taken place under the watch of a single president, Donald Trump. All amount to betrayal of the trust placed in him by the American people and bequeathed to him by those who labored and fought to create and preserve our system of government.

While Robert Mueller's report makes a compelling and, I

believe, irrefutable case that Trump and his associates know-
ingly collaborated with a foreign enemy in order to win the
presidency, and that they then repeatedly not only defended
that foreign power but rewarded it with benefits no other American president would ever have thought to bestow upon it, and
even left the door open to further attacks on our system in elections to come, there was more to his work than that. Because
in volume 2 of his report, he describes a systematic effort to
obstruct justice on the part of Donald Trump, which was not
only part of the defense of the Russians but which was, apart
from its intent, a serial, systematic abuse of power of a sort that
transcends the abuses of power cited in the impeachments of
Johnson, Nixon, and Clinton combined.

Mueller begins this section by noting and explaining why
he could not charge a sitting U.S. president with a crime. That is
not an accident. In the methodical construction of the Mueller
Report, the beginning, middle, and end of this volume document the reasons why, if that he had been able to charge Trump
with a crime, he would have. That crime would have been obstruction of justice.

The volume goes into great detail on eleven areas in which
potential instances of obstruction of justice by Trump were in-
vestigated by Mueller. These were, in the words of the report,
as follows:

- The campaign's response to reports about Russian
  support for Trump
- Conduct involving FBI Director Comey and Michael
  Flynn
- The president's reaction to the continuing Russia
  investigation

- The president's termination of Comey
- The appointment of a special counsel and efforts to remove him
- Efforts to curtail the special counsel's investigation
- Efforts to prevent the public disclosure of evidence
- Further efforts to have the attorney general take control of the investigation
- Efforts to have (White House counsel) McGahn deny that the president had ordered him to have the special counsel removed
- Conduct toward Flynn, Manafort, (and a name that was redacted citing "harm to an on-going matter)
- Conduct involving Michael Cohen

Mueller's report notes that while some of the president's behaviors were "facially lawful," he had "unique and powerful means of influencing official proceedings, subordinate officers, and potential witnesses—all of which is relevant to a potential obstruction-of-justice analysis." It goes on to note that while they were unable to conclusively prove underlying crimes (which, as noted earlier, was in part due to lack of cooperation with the investigation by the Trump team), obstruction of justice laws do not require the proof of such a crime.

Mueller goes on to address some of the ways Trump sought to intimidate or influence potential witnesses or the process of his case, by saying:

> *Third, many of the President's acts directed at witnesses, including discouragement of cooperation with the government and suggestions of possible future pardons, took place in pub-*

lic view. That circumstance is unusual, but no principle of
law excludes public acts from the reach of the obstruction
laws. If the likely effect of public acts is to influence witnesses
or alter their testimony, the harm to the justice system's in-
tegrity is the same.

It also notes that the president's intent shifted as the investigation moved from a phase in which he was told he was not a
target of its efforts to one in which he knew the special counsel
was weighing whether he had committed obstruction of justice.
This latter phase included "public attacks on the investigation,
non-public efforts to control it, and efforts in both public and
private to encourage witnesses not to cooperate with the investigation."

The report goes on to make the point that (despite statements from the president and his attorneys to the contrary,
statements echoing Nixon's "when the president does it . . . it
is not illegal" theory) that "the Constitution does not categorically and permanently immunize a President for obstructing
justice through the use of his Article II powers. The separation-
of-powers doctrine authorizes Congress to protect official
proceedings, including those of courts and grand juries, from
corrupt obstructive, acts regardless of their source." This point
is followed by perhaps the two most notable points in the report, drawn here from the executive summary prepared by
Mueller:

The conclusion that Congress may apply the obstruction laws
to the President's corrupt exercise of the powers of office ac-
cords with our constitutional system of checks and balances
and the principle that no person is above the law.

CONCLUSION

Because we determined not to make a traditional prosecuto-rial judgment, we did not draw ultimate conclusions about the President's conduct. The evidence we obtained about the President's actions and intent presents difficult issues that would need to be resolved if we were making a traditional prosecutorial judgment. At the same time, if we had confidence after a thorough investigation of the facts that the President clearly did not commit obstruction of justice, we would so state. Based on the facts and the applicable legal standards, we are unable to reach that judgment. Accordingly, while this report does not conclude the President committed a crime, it also does not exonerate him. [emphasis added]

Essentially, despite having accumulated masses of persuasive evidence that the president was guilty of obstruction of justice, Mueller and his team chose to punt the decision whether to act on that evidence over to the Congress, repository of Article I powers of oversight over the president. In his congressional testimony in the summer of 2019, Mueller repeated this conclusion and the effective charge to Congress.

While Trump's attorney general William Barr carried on the attempt to obstruct or at least obscure justice further by distorting Mueller's findings, the above paragraphs and the evidence underlying them was so compelling that they motivated over one thousand former prosecutors from both political parties—people who had served in every U.S. presidential administration since Eisenhower—to conclude that the president's conduct "trying to control and impede the investigation against the President by leveraging his authority over others—is similar to conduct we have seen charged against other public officials and people in powerful positions." They then go on to say "As former federal prosecutors, we recognize that prosecuting obstruction of justice cases is critical because unchecked obstruction—which allows intentional interference with criminal investigations to go unpunished—puts our whole system of justice at risk. We believe strongly that, but for the OLC memo, the overwhelming weight of professional judgment would come down in favor of prosecution for the conduct outlined in Mueller Report."

It was a compelling statement. And following Mueller's testimony to the House of Representatives in July 2019, it produced a reaction from the Congress. Within days of Mueller's presentation, a majority of Democrats in the House had determined to support an impeachment investigation of the potential charges suggested by Mueller in both volumes of his report, because, as we have noted earlier, the standard for impeachment of a president is different from the more narrow technical standards of the law.

That said, Trump's assault on the public trust is not simply grave from a constitutional or ethical perspective, it is breathtaking in its scope.

We have focused here primarily around the issues of the Russia affair and obstruction of justice, much as the Mueller investigation did. But it is already a matter of fact that Trump's alleged and proven abuses extend much further. The Mueller investigation spawned fourteen other cases to the rest of the Department of Justice, cases currently still open (in some cases despite the best efforts of Attorney General Barr to shut them down.) Then, in the fall of 2019, the Ukraine case, which was the proximate cause for the decision of the House of Representatives to investigate and ultimately impeach Trump took center stage.

THE THIRD AMERICAN PRESIDENT IN HISTORY
TO BE IMPEACHED

We have described the issues associated with the case here. But having reviewed past impeachments, it is illuminating to look more closely at the specifics of Trump's case before the House.

The Ukraine case broke quickly. The existence of the whistle-blower complaint against Trump was revealed in *The Washington Post* and other media on September 5, 2019. By September 24, Speaker of the House Nancy Pelosi, who had been reluctant to proceed with an impeachment case in the wake of the Mueller Report findings, announced that six commitees of the House of Representatives would initiate an impeachment inquiry. The Permanent Select Committee on Intelligence, the Oversight Committee, and the Foreign Affairs Committee began deposing witnesses within weeks. By October 31, by a vote of 232 to 196, following party lines with one Democrat voting with the GOP and one former Republican voting with the Democrats, Congress approved a resolution authorizing the impeachment inquiry.

November 2019 saw testimony from a number of individuals close to the Ukraine case, including former ambassador to Ukraine Marie Yovanovitch, then current acting Ambassador to Ukraine William Taylor, U.S. ambassador to the EU Gordon Sondland, former NSC senior director Fiona Hill, NSC staffer Lt. Col. Alexander Vindman, and a number of other former diplomats and White House staffers. The story they told was consistent. Beginning with the inauguration of Ukraine's new president, Volodymyr Zelensky, in the spring of 2019, Trump had sought via his emissaries—including Sondland, diplomat Kurt Volcker, and Energy Secretary Rick Perry, as well as Giuliani, Parnas, Fruman, and others—to pressure Zelensky into publicly announcing an investigation into former vice president and potential Trump 2020 rival Joe Biden and his son Hunter and their involvement with a Ukrainian energy company, Burisma, as well as into reports that Ukraine rather than Russia was somehow behind the interference in the 2016 elections. Ultimately, to do this, Trump ordered $391 million in aid that the Congress had approved for Ukraine to be withheld. He also dangled but did not deliver on hosting Zelensky at the White House, a meeting that would have given important validation to the new president (a former comedian who was seeking to establish himself as a strong leader for the country both in terms of fighting corruption and in terms of standing up to the Russian-backed invasion of his country). The details of the case had been brought to light by a whistle-blower report from an intelligence agency employee who had heard of Trump's July 25, 2019, call with Zelensky in which he asked Zelensky for a "favor" in a way that seemed to be conditioning the aid on its delivery. It was later learned that the Office of Management and Budget had stopped the distribution of the aid money despite protests from both the Department of Defense and the State Department, and it seemed that decision came directly from the president.

At the heart of the case was trying to determine whether Trump had explicitly predicated releasing the payments (which the Government Accountability Office, a nonpartisan Congressional oversight organization, later concluded amounted to a crime in and of itself) and the Oval Office meeting on the announcement of the investigations. Sondland testified that in his view there was a clear "quid pro quo." Acting White House Chief of Staff Mick Mulvaney, who also was the director of the Office of Management and Budget, confirmed this conclusion in a press conference on October 17, 2019, when he said that the aid had in fact been in part predicated on an investigation into "corruption related to the DNC server." When asked if this amounted to a quid pro quo, he acknowledged it did and suggested that this was how foreign policy was done and that those who objected should "get over it."

On December 3, the Intelligence Committee, which had been given the lead in preparing a report into the hearings, voted 13 to 9 to adopt its report and submit it to the Judiciary Committee for consideration in formulating articles of impeachment. The heart of the case was framed as follows:

> *The impeachment inquiry has found that President Trump, personally and acting through agents within and outside the U.S. government, solicited the interference of a foreign government, Ukraine, to benefit his re-election.*

The Republican members of the committee objected vigorously, arguing that there was no direct evidence of wrongdoing, that no crime had been committed, that the whistle-blower should have been brought before the committee, that the rules of the hearings were unfair to the president and no case for impeachment had been made, that Trump had been acting within his prerogatives as president, and that investigating the Bidens for corruption or pursuing information on the theory regarding Ukraine and the 2016 election was perfectly appropriate presidential behavior. (Even though there was not one scintilla of evidence supporting an investigation into either matter.)

The Judiciary Committee began hearings on December 4 and by December 10 initiated the drafting of two articles of impeachment, one focusing on abuse of power and the other on obstruction of Congress. Voting along party lines on December 13, the committee voted to pass both articles by a vote of 23 to 17. The impeachment vote took place on the evening of December 18.

The article on abuse of power passed by a 230-to-197 vote, again with essentially each party voting as a block, embracing, as it were, alternative views of the universe. The obstruction of Congress article passed shortly later by a vote of 229 to 198.

The core text of the articles is as follows:

ARTICLE I: ABUSE OF POWER

In his conduct of the office of President of the United States— and in violation of his constitutional oath faithfully to execute the office of President of the United States and, to the best of his ability, preserve, protect, and defend the Constitution of the United States, and in violation of his constitutional duty to take care that the laws be faithfully executed—Donald J. Trump has abused the powers of the Presidency, in that:

Using the powers of his high office, President Trump solicited the interference of a foreign government, Ukraine, in the 2020 United States Presidential election. He did so through a scheme or course of conduct that included soliciting the Government of Ukraine to publicly announce investigations that would benefit his reelection, harm the election prospects of a political opponent, and influence the 2020 United States Presidential election to his advantage. President Trump also sought to pressure the Government of Ukraine to take these steps by conditioning official United States Government acts of significant value to Ukraine on its public announcement of the investigations. President Trump engaged in this scheme or course of conduct for corrupt purposes in pursuit of personal political benefit. In so doing, President Trump used the powers of the Presidency in a manner that compromised the national security of the United States and undermined the integrity of the United States democratic process. He thus ignored and injured the interests of the Nation.

President Trump engaged in this scheme or course of conduct through the following means:

(1) President Trump—acting both directly and through his agents Within and Outside the United States Government corruptly solicited the Government of Ukraine to publicly announce investigations into—

(A) a political opponent, former Vice President Joseph R. Biden; and

(B) a discredited theory promoted by Russia alleging that Ukraine—rather than Russia—interfered in the 2016 United States Presidential election.

(2) With the same corrupt motives, President Trump—acting both directly and through his agents within and outside the United States Government—conditioned two official acts on the public announcements that he had requested—

(A) the release of $391 million of United States taxpayer funds that Congress had appropriated on a bipartisan basis for the purpose of providing vital military and security assistance to Ukraine to oppose Russian aggression and which President Trump had ordered suspended; and

(B) a head of state meeting at the White House, which the President of Ukraine sought to demonstrate continued United States support for the Government of Ukraine in the face of Russian aggression.

(3) Faced with the public revelation of his actions, President Trump ultimately released the military and security assistance to the Government of Ukraine, but has persisted in openly and corruptly urging and soliciting Ukraine to undertake investigations for his personal political benefit.

These actions were consistent with President Trump's previous invitations of foreign interference in United States elections.

In all of this, President Trump abused the powers of the Presidency by ignoring and injuring national security and other vital national interests to obtain an improper personal political benefit. He has also betrayed the Nation by abusing his high office to enlist a foreign power in corrupting democratic elections.

Wherefore President Trump, by such conduct, has demonstrated that he will remain a threat to national security and the Constitution if allowed to remain in office, and has acted in a manner grossly incompatible with self-governance and the rule of law. President Trump thus warrants impeachment and trial, removal from office, and disqualification to hold and enjoy any Office of honor, trust, or profit under the United States.

ARTICLE II: OBSTRUCTION OF CONGRESS

In his conduct of the office of President of the United States and in violation of his constitutional oath faithfully to execute the office of President of the United States and, to the best of his ability, preserve, protect, and defend the Constitution of the United States, and in violation of his constitutional duty to take care that the laws be faithfully executed—Donald J. Trump has directed the unprecedented, categorical, and indiscriminate defiance of subpoenas issued by the House of Representatives pursuant to its "sole Power of Impeachment". President Trump has abused the powers of the Presidency in a manner offensive to, and subversive of, the Constitution, in that:

The House of Representatives has engaged in an impeachment inquiry focused on President Trump's corrupt solicitation of the Government of Ukraine to interfere in the 2020 United States Presidential election. As part of this impeachment inquiry, the Committees undertaking the investigation served subpoenas seeking documents and testimony deemed vital to the inquiry from various Executive Branch agencies and offices, and current and former officials.

In response, without lawful cause or excuse, President Trump directed Executive Branch agencies, offices, and officials not to comply with those subpoenas. President Trump thus interposed the powers of the Presidency against the lawful subpoenas of the House of Representatives, and assumed to himself functions and judgments necessary to the exercise of the "sole Power of Impeachment" vested by the Constitution in the House of Representatives.

President Trump abused the powers of his high office through the following means:

(1) Directing the White House to defy a lawful subpoena by withholding the production of documents sought therein by the Committees.

(2) Directing other Executive Branch agencies and offices to defy lawful subpoenas and withhold the production of documents and records from the Committees—in response to which the Department of State, Office of Management and Budget, Department of Energy, and Department of Defense refused to produce a single document or record.

(3) Directing current and former Executive Branch officials not to cooperate with the Committees—in response to which nine Administration officials defied subpoenas for testimony, namely John Michael "Mick" Mulvaney, Robert B. Blair, John A. Eisenberg, Michael Ellis, Preston Wells Griffith, Russell T. Vought, Michael Duffey, Brian McCormack, and T. Ulrich Brechbuhl.

These actions were consistent with President Trump's previous efforts to undermine United States Government investigations into foreign interference in United States elections.

Through these actions, President Trump sought to arrogate to himself the right to determine the propriety, scope, and nature of an impeachment inquiry into his own conduct, as well as the unilateral prerogative to deny any and all information to the House of Representatives in the exercise of its "sole Power of Impeachment". In the history of the Republic, no President has ever ordered the complete defiance of an impeachment inquiry or sought to obstruct and impede so comprehensively the ability of the House of Representatives to investigate "high Crimes and Misdemeanors". This abuse of office served to cover up the President's own repeated misconduct and to seize and control the power of impeachment—and thus to nullify a vital constitutional safeguard vested solely in the House of Representatives.

> *In all of this, President Trump has acted in a manner con-*
> *trary to his trust as President and subversive of constitutional*
> *government, to the great prejudice of the cause of law and jus-*
> *tice, and to the manifest injury of the people of the United States.*

The articles were presented to the Senate of the United
States, after a delay due to concerns House leadership had
over the fairness of likely Senate rules, on January 15, 2020.
The Senate trial began the following week. As described earlier, the Senate trial featured the House managers presenting
their case and the lawyers for the president, led by White House
Counsel Pat Cipollone and Trump's personal attorney Jay Seku-
low, seeking to reiterate the same counterarguments that had
been heard from Republican committee members in both the
House Intelligence and Judiciary hearings.

The trial was rocked by new revelations from both Parnas
and Bolton but Senate majority leader Mitch McConnell and the
GOP managed nonetheless to suppress motions to hear new
witnesses as a result. In fact, absent witnesses, the Senate sessions could hardly be called a trial at all. Instead, they were
a stage for partisan posturing—Democrats making the case
against Trump, Republicans deflecting those arguments. And in
the end, the decision to acquit Trump was made almost entirely
on a partisan basis—with the exception of one vote cast by Utah
senator and former GOP presidential candidate Mitt Romney to
convict Trump on the first of the articles of impeachment against
him, the one concerning Trump's abuse of power. Despite having
taken oaths to be impartial, there was never any surprise about
the outcome of the Trump case.

Trump declared that he was vindicated by the verdict much
as he had done in the wake of the Mueller Report. But he had

been damaged by the impeachment process and by its conclusion: half of all Americans believed he should be convicted and
removed from office (according to a Fox News poll), with only
44 percent believing he should be acquitted. Even more, almost
two-thirds of all Americans believed Trump was guilty of wrongdoing. There was a straightforward reason for that verdict in the
court of public opinion. Trump had indeed abused power and obstructed Congress. Not a single piece of exculpatory evidence was
presented on his behalf. And what is more, as Adam Schiff noted
during one of his impassioned and eloquent interventions, there
was no testimony that it was not in Trump's character to commit
such crimes because everyone knew that, in fact, it was a clear
expression of that character, a repeat of past behaviors that placed
his personal interests ahead of those of the American people, in
which he sought foreign interference to help win an election, in
which he operated in an underhanded way and then actively
sought to cover it up, in which he argued that as president he had
the right under Article II of the Constitution to do anything at all.

Therein lay Trump's other great betrayal and that of the
GOP on his behalf. It was a betrayal of the core ideas on which
the country was founded—that no man or woman is above the
law, that we are a nation of laws, and that our government is
comprised of co-equal branches that provide vital checks and
balances against one another. Trump, helped into office by a corrupt autocrat, Vladimir Putin, cozy with other corrupt autocrats
while in office, from Saudi Arabia's Mohammed bin Salman to
North Korea's Kim Jong-un, from Erdogan in Turkey to Duterte
in the Philippines to Bolsonaro in Brazil to Xi in China, actively
sought, with the assistance of his attorney general and the Senate
majority leader, to gain the unchecked, uncheckable power of an
autocrat himself. To the extent that this was in direct opposition

to the core principles on which America was founded and to the Constitution he took an oath to preserve, protect, and defend, this represented a profound betrayal by Trump, traitorous not in service of a foreign power but to ideas and principles foreign to the form of government the United States has enjoyed since our Constitution was ratified in 1789.

A PRESIDENTIAL RAP SHEET LIKE NO OTHER

To get a sense of the extent of Trump's betrayal of the trust and values of the American people, consider it in the context of prior abuses and the scandals of the past.

Jefferson, Hamilton, Jackson, Cleveland, Harding, and Clinton all were involved in notable sex scandals. Trump outdoes all those scandals added together. At least twenty-four women have accused Donald Trump of sexual misconduct dating back to the 1970s. These include at least two women who have accused him of rape—his ex-wife Ivana and journalist E. Jean Carroll. (Ivana later withdrew her charge.) He has also been sued in the past in conjunction with an allegation that he raped a thirteen-year-old girl and he has been condemned for his exploits alongside noted child predator Jeffrey Epstein, who died in August of 2019 in a federal jail cell while awaiting trial.

The sex scandals associated with Trump are more than merely repulsive—although they are clearly that—and beyond what should be disqualifying for a public official or frankly anyone in a position of trust of any sort. They have been the source of additional crimes. Trump has been cited as a coconspirator with Michael Cohen in committing violations of federal election laws due to hush-money payments to two women with whom he had extramarital affairs, Stephanie Clifford and Karen McDougal. The payments came in the waning hours of the 2016 election campaign, when Trump feared disclosure of his relationships would damage his election chances. (If Robert Mueller were truly looking for a way to value the assistance provided by the Russians, he might have considered it was worth $150,000 to Trump to silence Clifford alone. Of course, as noted earlier, the many tens of millions or more dollars of value the Russians have received in quid pro quo policy gifts since their intervention on Trump's behalf is another way of establishing what their efforts were worth in Trump's eyes. Consider just how much Russia would have had to pay a Washington lobbying firm like that of Paul Manafort just to get them to try to encourage such outcomes.)

Michael Cohen pleaded guilty to the hush-money crimes, while Trump, again, remains uncharged as president. But he is named in the court documents as Cohen's coconspirator. He broke the law.

We have seen the financial crimes committed from revolutionary days onward through to Warren Harding and the Teapot Dome Scandal. But few compare with those with which Trump has been accused or for which he is under investigation. New York State shut down the Trump Foundation for financial violations. The Trump Inaugural Committee is under investigation for financial improprieties. *The New York Times* revealed in October 2018 that Trump—who it estimates received $413 million from his father despite long having claimed that he was more or less self-made—achieved much of his wealth through systematic tax fraud, maneuvers that used sham corporations to mask gifts totaling $1 billion from Trump's parents to him and his siblings. While these cases have yet to be brought against Trump, it is worth noting that his sister stepped down from the federal judiciary in the wake of the *Times* story, and that Trump has vigorously fought to keep his taxes from public view.

That fight has included Trump's Treasury Department withholding his tax returns from Congress despite the law requiring the Internal Revenue Service to turn over the returns of any taxpayer to the chairman of the House Ways and Means Committee. The House of Representatives issued a subpoena for the returns, and when that was ignored, they filed a lawsuit (pending at the time of this writing) seeking to compel the administration to comply. Failing to comply with subpoenas from the Congress is, in fact, another pattern within this administration, one that echoes precisely the reasons that Andrew Johnson was impeached in 1868.

It is worth noting as well that just as past administrations have had scandals resulting in the resignation or firing and subsequent prosecution of senior officials, Trump has seen more such turnover and more prosecutions in his first three years in office than any president in American history. Cabinet secretaries Alexander Acosta, Ryan Zinke, Jeff Sessions, Scott Pruitt, Kirstjen Nielsen, and Tom Price have resigned while investigations or controversies swirled about them. There have been investigations launched into the fact that the White House provided security clearances to twenty-five individuals who had a "wide range of serious disqualifying issues," including drug use and criminal conduct. Clearances were regularly provided over the objections of professional security staff, including the clearances of both Trump's daughter Ivanka and her husband, also a Trump senior advisor, Jared Kushner. It was a security scandal in the White House that was without precedent. And likely in the wake of Trump's first term as more information comes to light about his mishandling of the 2020 pandemic, of his denying or delaying aid to "blue" states, or of other missteps, more investigations appear inevitable.

The business affairs of Trump, Ivanka, Kushner, and the Trump family have also resulted in growing scrutiny beyond what was attendant to the Mueller investigation. Conflicts of interest by the Trumps in not just Russia but Saudi Arabia, the United Arab Emirates, China, Malaysia, and elsewhere have become the subject of congressional investigation. But lawsuits citing the president's violations of the Constitution's Emoluments Clause may present an even more egregious crime on the part of the president. The clause prohibits federal officeholders from receiving, without Congress's approval, "any present, Emolument, Office, or Title, of any kind whatever, from any King, Prince, or foreign State." Trump-owned enterprises, from the Trump International Hotel in Washington, D.C., to Trump Tower in New York, have clients that are foreign governments, some of which stepped up their business activities in these entities after Trump took office. The president is also precluded by the Constitution from receiving any compensation from the United States or any state while serving as president, but again, the federal government has spent massively in Trump properties, thereby enriching the president, during his presidency and presumably at his direction. Questions regarding his potential violation of both clauses were raised in 2019 when Trump announced that the 2020 summit of the leaders of the world's seven largest industrial economies would occur at the Trump National Doral resort in Miami—a position he later stepped away from under pressure due to the egregiousness of the self-dealing that would have been involved.

In short, if you take all of the great instances of abuse of the public trust in U.S. history and add to them all of the presidential scandals, they would be exceeded in number and severity by the actions of just Trump and those closest to him. If you were to summarize the abuses cited in the articles of impeachment of Andrew Johnson, Richard Nixon, and Bill Clinton—for failing to follow federal law, failing to honor their commitments to preserve, protect, and defend the laws of the United States, for ridiculing the Congress and treating it with disrespect, for obstruction of justice, for abuse of power, and for perjury— you would find that Trump has committed them all, often to a more pronounced degree than his predecessors. His multiple instances of obstruction of justice outstrip Nixon's many times over. His abuses of the Congress are greater than Johnson's. His dishonesty—remember this is a man who has lied more than sixteen thousand times since taking office, including in some instances misleading federal authorities or promoting deception in others—makes Clinton's pale in comparison.

For every flaw in the characters of Trump's predecessors, he has presented not just many more defects but a willingness to embrace those deficits, to flaunt them, and to seek to capitalize on them while in office. And as we have seen, he has done so at the level of the highest crimes possible for a president of the United States to commit and of the lowest misdemeanors.

The only question that remains is, Will he be held accountable by the Congress, the courts, or now or later by the American people?

7

THE ULTIMATE BETRAYAL OF THE
SPIRIT OF AMERICA'S FOUNDERS

THE RISE OF A GENERATION OF
REPUBLICAN MONARCHS?

*The general Government . . . can never be in danger of degen-
erating into a monarchy, an Oligarchy, an Aristocracy . . . so
long as there shall remain any virtue in the body of the People.*

—George Washington

As we consider these scandals from throughout our history, it is
impossible not to be struck by how regularly we face them and
how common some of their attributes seem to be—from greed
to abuse of power. But we also must be impressed by the resil-
ience of the U.S. system and the fact that typically, if not always,
when called upon to place the rule of law above the interests of
an individual or a party, the country and those within its positions of trust have placed the preservation of public trust first.

At least that has been the case thus far. As of this writing, it
is far from certain that will be the case with regard to the abuses
caused by Donald Trump and his administration.

While the most egregious of these, the ones that have earned the greatest amount of attention during Trump's first term, may have been those associated with the Trump-Russia scandal, they are certainly not the only instances of Trump and those around him violating the standards that in the past would have triggered consideration of his removal from office or other forms of prosecution. While thirty-four people were indicted in the Mueller probe and thus far seven have been convicted, there remain a number of open cases against Trump that fall into the different categories of abuse of the public trust that have marked the past scandals associated with the country's highest office: abuse of power—notably obstruction of justice, but also including failure to uphold a president's oath of office, financial corruption, and sex or other personal forms of scandalous behavior.

While the Ukraine case resulted in the impeachment of Trump and two of his operatives in that case, Parnas and Fruman, have been indicted on other grounds while a third, Giuliani, is reportedly under scrutiny, what looms largest is that Trump was acquitted, that he got away with it—with the assistance of rather than under pressure from his Department of Justice. The DoJ, to pick just one example, sought to quash the whistle-blower report that brought the Ukraine extortion to light. The nature of the very role of the Department of Justice has changed under this administration. All sense of independence, propriety, and service to the Constitution has been lost. In another time perhaps this would trigger not just a reassessment but the prosecution of those who were responsible for these serial gross miscarriages of justice. But for now, it leaves us with more questions than answers—not just about the Ukraine case or its ties to the Russia case or the manifold crimes either may contain (the entire Russia scandal is a matryoshka doll of crimes and abuses; breaking each new one open reveals others within it), but to how these crimes are affecting the way the U.S. government works and whether either democracy or justice is likely to survive in the United States.

Needless to say, the performance of the U.S. Senate in the impeachment trial only compounded these concerns. They set rules not for a fair trial but to ensure Trump's acquittal regardless of the underlying evidence. Cases were presented before the question of whether new witnesses or evidence should be sought was even considered—despite the fact that in literally all the impeachments in U.S. history (including not just presidents but judges), witnesses and new evidence were part of the proceedings. The deck was stacked against hearing from witnesses and, as noted earlier, none were even called to appear.

While the title of this book is *Traitor*, and the term naturally conjures thoughts about adhering to or aiding and abetting foreign enemies, as we have seen, the term is not exclusively used in that context. From the Whiskey Rebellion to Fries's uprising, from John Brown to Walter Allen, and of course in the context of the Civil War, we have even seen the term "treason" used to address cases in which the issue was disloyalty to national or state governments and posing a perceived threat to those entities. That is consistent with the roots of the idea of the crime in English common law. Recalling that the founders drew the language concerning treason in our Constitution from the law on that subject promulgated by Edward III of England during the fourteenth century, it is worth noting that none of the key components of that law were actually associated with foreign enemies. They referred, in fact, to more perceived domestic threats, including levying war against the king, adhering to the enemies of the king, supporting them, "compassing or imagining the death of the king," or even having sex with certain ladies of the royal household.

In short, the original concept of treason centered on what was perceived as the worst possible crime against the state: undertaking acts that threatened its very existence (which, at the time of Edward, was encompassed in and flowed from the person of the king). Today the state is embodied in the Constitution—to which the president takes an oath and which he or she promises to preserve, protect, and defend—and the institutions, principles, and laws established within it. Central to these is the concept that no individual is above the law, that, indeed, power flows from the people who are empowered with guiding their own destinies and to whom all in even the most senior positions of power report. To betray that principle is perhaps above all others a betrayal of the central rationale for the American state. But to undertake to undermine or attack any of the institutions, principles, and laws contained within the Constitutions or its legal legacy within our system, whether promulgated by the judicial, legislative, or executive branches of our government, is certainly the equivalent of the kind of attack on the state envisioned within the statute of 25 Edward III (1350).

Indeed, in the world in which we live today, we might see the Constitution's protections against such attacks on the state as antiquated and wanting revision. This is not just because threats can emanate from many sources. That has always been the case. It is that the words of Article III, Section 3, Clause 1 of the Constitution have been so narrowly interpreted that they no longer can extend to the nature of modern conflict in which war is often not officially declared and yet a state of enmity exists in which a foreign power may seek to damage us and in which attacks often come in peacetime and in forms unimagined by our predecessors—such as those associated with cyber attack or information warfare.

That said—especially given the low likelihood of amending the Constitution at this time (more's the pity since it contains a number of other anachronisms that need addressing, like the existence of the Electoral College)—we as citizens need to recognize those crimes and abuses that are essential to the preservation of that which is best about our system of government. None is more central to these than this idea of ensuring that no one is above the law. It is the reason the country was established, the reason we rejected the British monarchy and the rule of George III. Throughout our history we have struggled with this idea. For much of that history we debated whose law that referred to, whether in fact state governments or the federal government was the ultimate sovereign. More recently, however, we have been forced to revisit the idea of whether we have created institutions or structures that place a president, and perhaps even those close to him, above the law. The Office of Legal Counsel memo that was an impediment to Mueller's charging the president with a crime is such a development. Though not a law passed by Congress, and though completely inconsistent with the Constitution and the principles underlying it, we have for decades now adopted a view within the executive branch and accepted by the Congress that the only way to charge a president with a crime, to hold him or her accountable for abuses, is via the mechanism of impeachment by the House and removal from office by the Senate. Unfortunately, what that mechanism does, however, is grant immunity to any president who controls a sufficient number of senators to foreclose the possibility of a two-thirds vote to convict.

In other words, if one party can control thirty-four seats in the Senate and that party protects an occupant of the White House of similar beliefs, that president is, in fact, beyond the reach of the law. He or she is, in fact, precisely the kind of monarch the founders were seeking to overthrow. That president can lie, steal, twist the law, enforce laws selectively, and ignore the will of the public, the Congress, and even arguably the courts without the citizens of the country having any effective form of redress.

Compound that fact with the provisions within the Constitution that grant two Senate seats per state, thus giving each state regardless of its population equal representation and thereby giving the people of less-populous states disproportionate representations, and you have a situation in which one party can gain effective immunity for presidents affiliated with it by winning a comparative minority of American voters. That is the situation we find ourselves in today, with the GOP and its grip on "red states" that happen to generally correspond to those less-populated yet nonetheless super-constitutionally empowered states discussed here.

This even seems to present the possibility of an ideological bias within our system, given that the inhabitants of the less-populated states, less exposed to the diversity of urban areas and the familiarity with and tolerance of people of different origins and beliefs that brings, tend to be more "conservative." That is to say, they tend to be wary of foreigners, of people

THE ULTIMATE BETRAYAL 211

who look different, of the power of those in cities and thus in government—all foundational ideas of Trumpism or the right wing in America today.

What is more, their relative power is likely to grow in the years ahead. As scholar Norman Ornstein has pointed out "By 2040 or so, 70 percent of Americans will live in 15 states. Meaning the 30 percent will choose 70 senators. And the 30 percent will be older, whiter, more rural, more male than the 70 percent." The flip side is that 70 percent of the country will only get thirty seats in the Senate, not enough to muster the thirty-four votes needed to defeat motions requiring a two-thirds majority.

In other words, take the Constitution plus the Office of Legal Counsel memorandum on why a sitting president cannot be charged with a crime, plus the effective control of the United States Senate (the convicting body in the only legal mechanism available to hold a president in check), and you have a formula for an era of Republican or Trumpist kings and queens, individuals who will effectively be beyond the reach of the law and able to selectively honor and enforce the laws they choose.

FLATTERING THE PREJUDICES OF THE PEOPLE

When viewed in the context of history, Trump and our era present us with plenty of cause for concern. That said, there is some cause for hope. Our institutions remain intact if, to date, underused to address the threat of a man like the one who, at the time of this writing, occupies the White House. Further, our press and many from every level and corner of our society have shown the character and courage to call out Trump and to challenge his assault on our values and our system of government.

One such set of voices has come from so-called Never Trumpers and other former members of Republican administrations and Republican leaders who have been critical of the president when it has been called for. That includes commentators and observers like George Will, David Brooks, Bret Stephens, Max Boot, Nicolle Wallace, and William Kristol. In an article in the conservative-leaning *Washington Examiner* in 2018, Kristol invoked again the voice of Alexander Hamilton to discuss the character of the president. He quoted from Federalist No. 68:

> *The process of election affords a moral certainty, that the office of President will never fall to the lot of any man who is not in an eminent degree endowed with the requisite qualifications. Talents for low intrigue, and the little arts of popularity, may alone suffice to elevate a man to the first honors in a single State; but it will require other talents, and a different kind of merit, to establish him in the esteem and confidence of the whole Union, or of so considerable a portion of it as would be necessary to make him a successful candidate for the distinguished office of President of the United States. It will not be too strong to say, that there will be a constant probability of seeing the station filled by characters pre-eminent for ability and virtue.*

This is, of course, an optimistic moment in an essay designed to promote the new Constitution to the people. But as Kristol notes, Hamilton was not blind to the threats that exist in a democracy. Several years afterward he wrote:

> *The truth unquestionably is, that the only path to a subversion of the republican system of the Country is, by flattering*

the prejudices of the people, and exciting their jealousies and apprehensions, to throw affairs into confusion, and bring on civil commotion. . . . When a man unprincipled in private life desperate in his fortune, bold in his temper, possessed of considerable talents, having the advantage of military habits—despotic in his ordinary demeanour—known to have scoffed in private at the principles of liberty—when such a man is seen to mount the hobby horse of popularity—to join in the cry of danger to liberty—to take every opportunity of embarrassing the General Government & bringing it under suspicion—to flatter and fall in with all the nonsense of the zealots of the day—It may justly be suspected that his object is to throw things into confusion that he may "ride the storm and direct the whirlwind."

While this is not the "only path" to subversion of our system, as we have seen over time, it is certainly one of them and one that resonates today despite Trump's deficiencies in terms of "the advantage of military habits." The risks to a democracy of the elevation of a leader of bad character who knows how to work the system—by flattering "the prejudices of the people, and exciting their jealousies and apprehensions"—are clear. Roughly 150 years after Hamilton, they were described in somewhat more acid terms by the great American journalist and commentator H. L. Mencken, when he wrote, "As democracy is perfected, the office [of president] represents, more and more closely, the inner soul of the people. We move toward a lofty ideal. On some great and glorious day the plain folks of the land will reach their heart's desire at last, and the White House will be adorned by a downright moron."

Mencken wrote that in 1920 during the election that would

elevate Warren G. Harding to the presidency. But his views went beyond that prophecy to reveal a deeper understanding of the risks of populism. He wrote of the average citizen, that instead of embracing his freedoms, "He longs for the warm, reassuring smell of the herd, and is willing to take the herdsman with it," as well as, "The demagogue who is one who preaches doctrines he knows to be untrue to men he knows to be idiots."

In the early days of the Trump administration, I wrote for *Foreign Policy* magazine something that picks up on these themes:

> *Donald Trump, champion and avatar of the shallow state, has won power because his supporters are threatened by what they don't understand, and what they don't understand is almost everything. Indeed, from evolution to data about our economy to the science of vaccines to the threats we face in the world, they reject vast subjects rooted in fact in order to have reality conform to their worldviews. They don't dig for truth; they skim the media for anything that makes them feel better about themselves. To many of them, knowledge is not a useful tool but a cunning barrier elites have created to keep power from the average man and woman.*

While this may sound like just another condemnation of "the deplorables" from someone comfortably living in an ivory tower (and note that I am currently writing this from an apartment located atop a pizzeria in Greenwich Village, which is not the same thing no matter what Breitbart might tell you), it is not. It is a desire to zero in on the fact that the first war waged by demagogues is against the truth, as sage observers from Hannah Arendt to Michiko Kakutani have reminded us.

After all, it is only by creating the idea of fake news that a man who has endured six bankruptcies can persuade voters he was a master businessman; a man whose finances were unknown but who, according to *The New York Times*, during one year in the 1990s lost more money than any other human being in America, can sell himself, without a shred of evidence, as a billionaire; a man without a moment of his life spent in public service can persuade millions that he cares about their plight; or a man without any policy competencies can convince voters of his competency to govern.

As it happens, the technique is also useful when discrediting enemies and critics. As it also happens, it is the stock-in-trade of many authoritarian governments and has been a special favorite of the leaders in the Kremlin for almost one hundred years, practiced with special skill by its information warriors, the Russian frontline troops deployed to assist Trump in 2016.

What it leads to, of course, is the elevation of a man who was a traitor from before he took office and has been an ever-greater catastrophe as president with every day he has been in office. This was, it must be remembered, the most important goal of the Russian intervention—to elevate a man and propel a movement that would divide and weaken their principal rival, the United States.

We have not discussed here the manifold failures of Trump and Trump administration policies that compound the damage done by his abuses of his office. Many of these have been far greater in their negative consequences for the United States and the world than even his wrongdoing or his utter lack of a moral compass. Whether it has been his racism, which has divided the country; or his racist policies, which have targeted and punished

Muslims, Latinos, other people of color and all immigrants; or his systematic dismantling of environmental protections—we have seen bad policies with dark motives supported by a rejection of fact and science. We have seen the dealmaker foiled in trade deal after trade deal, and the master negotiator who has alienated virtually every ally America has in the world. We have seen the undoing of the post–World War II international order (as noted before to suit the goals of the Russians) as well as a precipitous decline in U.S. leadership (as noted before to also suit the goals of the Russians). We have seen a man championing the cause of the disenfranchised who elected him to create tax breaks for the top 1 percent and corporate interests. We have also seen the serial defense of the indefensible, from Trumpian lies to Trumpian abuses; from the death of innocents through negligence in Puerto Rico to the death of innocents and the suffering of thousands of others due to human-rights-violating policies on the border; from the embrace of autocrats to the celebration and rewarding of the murderers of Jamal Khashoggi and those in China who have put Muslims in concentration camps in Xinjiang Province, which rivals the scale of what the Nazis did; from those in Turkey and the Philippines who have gutted democracy to an autocrat who runs a slave state in North Korea that continues to build nuclear weapons targeting America and our allies.

Each of these, too, are among the crimes of Trump, but they are also the consequences of a movement that has devalued truth and sought to exploit the fears and divisions within our society, just as Hamilton predicted might be done. Therefore, we must recognize that to redress the crimes of Trump we cannot rely merely on courts, the Congress, or even elections—because we face the possibility of the weaponization of Trumpian techniques and values through the evolution of the threat posed by this one man and those close to him into the movement that he and many on America's far right seek to inspire.

NOT TRUMP BUT TRUMPISM

The problem, then, as I have written previously, is not Trump, it's Trumpism. It's not one man but the tens of millions who support him. If you dare not say that for fear of offending them, you also will not address the root causes of this societal disease. That's where our work must be done.

Those causes begin with alienation, fear, frustration, and anxiety. Those problems are exacerbated both by inherent prejudice and by the license to hate given by Trump, the GOP, evangelical ministers, Fox News, and the rest of the right-wing grievance-amplification machine.

What is different in the America of Trump is that hate has not only become more permissible in public, it is that the grievance machine has turned it into a bond among the disaffected, a rallying cry. It is no longer left versus right in America. It is the changing demographic and economic realities of twenty-first-century America versus what we might call the far white.

Racism has deep roots here, but we can only expect it to get worse during the years ahead, as we move toward a new reality a quarter century from now of being a minority-majority country. We must prepare for that and, indeed, we must recognize these coming changes for what they are—a realization of the promise of America, a strengthening of our country through diversity. But we also need to address as many of those other root-cause issues as we can.

Alienation comes from growing inequality in our society

and the concentration of hugely disproportionate power in the hands of the few. Fear comes from lying awake at night wondering if a job will be lost to progress or new markets or to the new people in town. Frustration comes from a Washington, D.C., that is hugely dysfunctional and profoundly corrupt—from self-dealing leaders whose promises, like Trump's to his base, are not only never fulfilled, they are actually lies hiding further abuses to come. Anxiety comes when all these things lead to economic and social fragility as a permanent, worsening state of mind. Most Americans would be bankrupted by a minor illness, a bad toothache. Fewer and fewer believe that the future will be better for their children.

The majority among Americans are ill prepared for retirement and actually fear living longer lives because what those lives promise is not joy or hope but deepening poverty. These are big, deep problems. Indeed, they have been worsening for forty years in America. Democrats and Republicans both have made them worse. But the answers to these problems and others that feed our divide and the rise of Trumpism are clear. We need to provide the education that people need at affordable costs.

We need to pay teachers enough that the best and brightest are drawn to help prepare new generations for new challenges. We need to ensure that everyone has health care as a right and that no one fears medical bankruptcy due to an accident or needing costly medications. We need to rebuild our infrastructure and retool our workforce for the next century. We need to reboot our tax structure so the richest and biggest companies pay their share and government resources serve the people and not just big government contractors.

We need campaign finance reform that removes the control

of the government from the hands of the top 1 percent and special interests like the NRA and the fossil-fuel lobbies. We need
to protect the environment in which our children will live. None
of this is radical. All is doable.

Indeed, all is already supported by bipartisan majorities
of our population. Serving that bipartisan majority, that "New
American Majority," not only makes sound political sense, but it
will help fix what is broken in America—in the way democracy
intended it to.

This shift will put many at risk. Not just Trump and his
cronies, but Mitch McConnell and the massive establishment
behind them. They will fight. But this time they may well lose
because they have so destroyed their own credibility and so revealed their own vileness.

It can be done. But it cannot be done simply by defeating
Trump. That is not enough. He is a symptom, not the disease. If
he goes and these core problems and the far-right establishment
remains, we will only get worse in the years to come.

That is why the job of the country right now is more sweeping than merely addressing Trump's crimes or beating in the
next election the most corrupt, despicable, incompetent, disloyal
president in U.S. history. That truly is the easy part. It is not to
be minimized, but it cannot be the only goal. The real job is
making that next election and the years that follow it a water-
shed, when it is not Democrats versus Trump, not a partisan
issue, but when the polity returns to the business of doing what
a democracy should: being motivated by a new majority seeking
to set us on a new course for the rest of the twenty-first century,
to address deep-seated problems with commonsense solutions,
and to end up with a future that is even better than our past.

THE CASE AGAINST TRUMP

Ultimately, as I have noted, the case for or against Trump will not be made by lawyers or politicians or pundits but will be left to history and historians. We are, in fact, already getting a sense of what that case may be with early judgments from scholars. One 2018 poll of two hundred top political scientists, conducted every four years, rated Trump dead last among all U.S. presidents, even among self-identified conservatives who were polled. On a scale of 1–100, Trump's average score was 12.34. Ranked immediately above him, at second to last, was James Buchanan, whose administration witnessed the final descent of the United States into Civil War. In another poll, this one the sixth in a series conducted since 1982 by the Siena College Research Institute, 157 academics who were surveyed ranked Trump third worst following Andrew Johnson and Buchanan. Suffice it to say, it is not a good place to be three years into one's first term in office.

In the end, those rankings are because of the unprecedentedly wide range of bad policies, administrative failures, and abuses that we have chronicled here.

As I wrote in the summer of 2019 while reflecting on the outcome of the Mueller Report and the record of the Trump administration to date, it is hard to pinpoint just one reason why the Trump administration has been such a catastrophe and, if history is any indicator, why it will likely be viewed that way by posterity.

Because in the end, Trump is a traitor. But it's not just his being a traitor. It's the obstruction of justice. But it's not just the obstruction of justice. It's the attacks on the rule of law. But it's not just the attacks on the rule of law. It's the assault on freedom of the press. But it's not just the assault on freedom of the press.

It's the pathological lying. But it's not just the pathological lying. It's the unfitness for office. But it's not just the unfitness for office. It's the incompetence. But it's not just the incompetence.

It's the racism. But it's not just the racism. It's sex crimes. But it's not just the sex crimes. It's the concentration camps along our southern border. But it's not just the concentration camps. It's the corruption. But it's not just the corruption.

It's the attacks on our most important allies and alliances. But it's not just the attacks on our most important allies and alliances. It's the systematic destruction of our environment. But it's not just the systematic destruction of our environment.

It's the violation of international treaties and agreements. But it is not just the violation of international treaties and agreements. It's the embrace of our enemies. But it is not just the embrace of our enemies.

It's the defense of murderous dictators. But it is not just the defense of murderous dictators. It is the serial undermining of our national security. But it is not just the serial undermining of our national security. It is the nepotism. But it's not just the nepotism.

It's the attacks on our federal law-enforcement and intelligence communities. But it is not just the attacks on our federal law-enforcement and intelligence communities. It's the fiscal recklessness. But it's not just the fiscal recklessness.

It's the degradation of the office and of public discourse in America. But it's not just the degradation of the office and of public discourse in America. It's the support of Nazis and white supremacists. But it's not just the support of Nazis and white supremacists.

It's the dead in Puerto Rico and in the wake of the coronavirus outbreak and at the border. But it's not just the dead in

Puerto Rico, in makeshift epidemic morgues, and at the border. It's turning the U.S. government into a criminal conspiracy to empower and enrich the president and his supporters.

But it's not just the turning of the U.S. government into a criminal conspiracy to empower and enrich the president and his supporters. It's the weaponization of politics in America to attack the weak. But it's not just the weaponization of American politics to attack the weak.

It's all these things together and the threat of worse to come. It is the damage that cannot be undone. It is the pathology that has overtaken our politics and our society, the revelation that 40 percent of the population—those whose loyalty to Trump never wavered despite continuing revelations about his crimes, his lies, his corruption, his abuses of power—and an entire political party are profoundly immoral.

It is a disease that has infected our system and is killing it. At the moment, we still have the wherewithal to fight back. But even those who recognize the dangers of this litany of crimes are proving too complacent, too inert in the face of this threat.

We find ourselves at one of those moments in the history of a country when there is a choice to be made, a choice between having a future and not, between growth and decay, between democracy and oligarchy, between what we dreamed of being and what even our founders feared we might become.

The litany of crises and crimes is so long that many Americans are becoming numb. You have heard of the fog of war. This is the "fog of Trump." The volume of wrongs becomes its own defense. Is the president accused of being a rapist? Well, then remind the American public he is a racist and they'll forget. (And some of them, it is clear, will support him more vigorously because of it.)

While history's verdict may already be clear, this is none-theless a moment for leaders to step up if we do not wish this dark moment to be a prelude to much worse. It is time to challenge each of these abuses via every legal means available. To organize and draw attention to them. To blow the whistle if you are in government and you are being asked to violate your oath. To resist and refuse to be complicit.

If you can't do those things that make your voice heard and join a movement, support a political candidate, donate money, register voters, fight voter suppression. But whatever you do, resist becoming numb. Resist the temptation to let the recitation of old crimes and new become a deadening drone. Everyone matters in times like these. Everyone must stand up for what is right. In our homes. In our schools. In the workplace. In our churches and synagogues and mosques.

We are approaching a great national decision—in the election ahead and in the years that immediately follow—about whether the American experiment will succeed or fail, whether this moment does what two world wars, a civil war, and countless past misjudgments and missteps could not.

We will make it together, resist, offer a better alternative, embrace that alternative and the best leaders we can find—or we will succumb, let the inertia of some among us mark the end of what for two and half centuries was an idea so compelling it inspired the world.

ACKNOWLEDGMENTS

Any book—of any length—is in my experience a far more collaborative enterprise than the single name on the cover may indicate. That has certainly been the case with regard to this book as well. People say writing is a lonely business, and at times it is. But it also brings you in contact with great people, brilliant minds, and opens up new worlds for the fortunate author. Who in this case is me.

I must begin by thanking my editor on this book, Stephen S. Power, and his colleagues at Thomas Dunne Books at St. Martin's Press, notably, of course, Tom Dunne. Stephen, who had the lead on this project there, was not only extraordinarily patient with me as events kept overtaking key elements of this narrative, but he was also an enthusiastic and well-informed partner in helping to shape that narrative.

The person who brought me into contact with Stephen is my agent, Esmond Harmsworth. Esmond has been my guide and wise counsel since I graduated from doing more "academic" books and monographs to "bigger" books and, frankly, I neither could have nor would have done any of them without him.

I also want to thank, as ever, my colleagues at the Carnegie Endowment for International Peace (despite what this book taught me about Elihu Root). Most notable among them was the president of the endowment, a man who is a foreign policy inspiration and mentor to me (despite being exactly the same age as I am), and that is Ambassador Bill Burns. Bill is perhaps the most distinguished career diplomat the U.S. Foreign Service has produced in the past forty years, certainly one of the very best, and, as it happens, is also brilliant and funny, and much of what is in this book was initially hashed out in conversations with him.

Also essential in that regard have been my colleagues at TRG Media, the little company I have where we produce the podcasts *Deep State Radio, National Security Magazine, Unredacted*, and *DSR Live,* as well as events and other content at our website TheDSRNetwork.com. Foremost among my colleagues there is my partner in the venture, our chairman, Bernard Schwartz. Bernard has had a vision of us as being a potentially influential source of political, foreign policy, and national security information since our founding, and despite the odds, he has helped us become one. Similarly, I am deeply grateful to our president there, Chris Cotnoir, with whom I have worked since my days at *Foreign Policy,* and to our vice president, Stacie Williams.

At both Carnegie and TRG, the lead researcher on this project has been Staley Smith. Staley did a fantastic job scouring sources for the history included here and keeping up with the rapidly growing library of books relating to Trump, his rise, and what one can only hope will be his fall.

One of the great pleasures of my life during the past several years has been working with my collaborators on Deep State Radio. Not only have they been great sources of knowledge and insight, they are also great friends. At the core are Rosa Brooks and Kori Schake, without whom Deep State Radio would not exist. Kori, deputy director general of the International Institute for Strategic Studies and permanent holder of the "Tiara of Optimism," and Rosa, the Scott K. Ginsburg Professor of Law and Policy at Georgetown University Law Center and lifetime recipient of the "Thorny Crown of Entropy," are among the two most brilliant people I know and, despite their many successes, have never lost their great senses of humor. Also part of the core team at DSR are two of my oldest friends in D.C., both of whom would be quick to point out that they are actually younger than me, David Sanger of *The New York Times* and Ed Luce of the *Financial Times*. In addition to their work on the show, both have helped me think through this book and kept me from making more great errors of judgment and conception than I did.

Others who have played a central role participating in our shows and thus contributed to the book because we regularly discussed the topics that ended up being covered here include my very smart partner on the *DSR Live* podcasts, Ryan Goodman, the Anne and Joel Ehrenkranz Professor of Law at NYU School of Law and also coeditor of JustSecurity.org, and regular guests Evelyn Farkas of the German Marshall Fund of the United States and Joe Cirincione of the Ploughshares Fund. Guests who participated in on-air discussions that fed directly into this book and to whom I am therefore immensely grateful include but are not limited to: Max Bergmann, Max Boot, Emily Brandwin, Rep. David Cicilline, Lt. Gen. James Clapper, Rep. Ted Deutch, Gen. Michael Hayden, Susan Hennessey, Lt. Gen. Mark Hertling, Fred Hochberg, Molly Jong-Fast, Rep. Ted Lieu, Harry Litman, Barbara McQuade, Michael Morell, Rep. Jerrold Nadler, Ben Pauker, Katie Phang, Philippe Reines, Laura Rosenberger, Rep. Adam Schiff, Jake Sullivan, Rep. Eric Swalwell, Laurence Tribe, Joyce Vance, Sharon Weinberger, and Ben Wittes.

To the four dozen individuals who spoke to me on background or off the record for this project, I also appreciate your time and your input.

On each of the books I have done, there are several long-standing friends with whom I talk because I always come away with better ideas than I went in with, and who always have been incredibly generous with their time. They include Tom Friedman, Jeffrey Garten, and Bob Hormats.

That said, everything I do in my life, I do for my family. They are my inspiration, my joy, a constant source of pride, comfort, humor, and genius. This of course, includes my sister and brother and their families.

Naturally, there is a special category of appreciation reserved for my two magnificent daughters, Joanna and Laura, who every day surpass what I thought was possible in terms of the joy a father could derive from having such children, well, any children, really. They are endless sources of pleasure and the dearest of the dear dears the world could produce.

Finally, last on this list but first in terms of the support I received from her daily is my wife, Carla Dirlikov Canales. I never imagined I would be so lucky as to find a love and a partner in everything, like her. In all of our adventures around the world and at home with our dog and research assistant, Grizzly, she fills me with joy and excitement for what tomorrow may hold. I love her with all my heart and am forever grateful to have her in my life.

INDEX